Robert DeNiro
and
The Fireman

Robert DeNiro
and
The Fireman

Bill Cosgrove

Rutledge Books, Inc. Bethel, CT

Rutledge Books, Inc.
8 F.J. Clarke Circle, Bethel, CT 06801

Manufactured in the United States of America

Cataloging in Publication Data
Cosgrove, Bill
    Robert DeNiro and the fireman / Bill Cosgrove
        p. cm.
    ISBN 1-887750-63-0
    1. Chicago (Ill.)-Biography. 2. Motion pictures-Biography.
3. Motion picture Actors and actresses.

920.71   97-68318

Dedication

Edward M. Cosgrove

Elizibeth Cosgrove

James P. Cosgrove

ROBERT DENIRO

18 October 1991

To Whom It May Concern;

I met Bill Cosgrove in July of 1990 when I
began production on the movie "Backdraft."
My character in this film was a Chicago Fire
Investigator.

Bill helped me research the part and escorted
me to actual fires in the Chicago area where
we went through the standard procedure followed
by a Fire Investigator.

Bill's special abilities are invaluable. He
conducted himself well both personally and
professionally.

I felt he would be a great asset to the
production, so he was hired as my technical
advisor. In addition, he was cast in an on
camera role in "Backdraft."

It is my opinion, based on the time I spent
with him and by observing the way he performed
on camera, that he could have a career as an
actor and technical advisor.

Sincerely,

Robert DeNiro

Acknowledgments

Susan Cosgrove	My Wife
Elizabeth Kirby	My Sister
Patrick Cosgrove	My Brother
William Alletto	My Friend
Mary Norton	My Friend
Kevin McCarthy	My Friend
Paul Salack	My Friend

Thank you all for your help, love, and support. I would not have been able to make it to the finish without you.

Thank you,
Bill Cosgrove

Introduction

In less than a year, two major events occurred that have changed the course of my life. One of these events was very good, and the other was very bad.

I am a person who likes good things, so I will tell what the good thing was that happened first.

The movie *Backdraft* was filmed in Chicago, and was a story about the Chicago Fire Department. It was about two brothers who were Chicago firefighters, a corrupt Chicago politician and a fire department arson investigator. That arson investigator was portrayed by none other than the great actor, Mr. Robert DeNiro.

Because of my fire department position as a fire investigator with the Chicago Fire Department, I was hired as a personal technical advisor on fire/arson investigation to Mr. DeNiro. Together, we worked for some forty-nine days. It was a tremendous experience that was mutually beneficial. When the part of the arson investigator was completed on October 8, 1990, Mr. DeNiro and I parted good friends...something that usually does not occur between technical advisor and actor.

The second event that occurred was very bad and almost took my life. I was critically injured in a motor vehicle accident in which I was thrown through the windshield and out onto Interstate 55. As a result of this accident, I fractured my back, my thoracic vertebrae number three, experiencing almost total evulsion of my right ear and the fracture of six ribs.

To recover from these injuries I needed the support of my family and friends, and I did get that support. My family and friends stayed by my side all the time. I received flowers from Ron Howard, William Baldwin and, yes, Mr. Robert DeNiro also.

Mr. DeNiro called me often, both in the hospital and at home, and visited me at my home on several occasions.

I would like to share with you what it was like to be a technical advisor to Mr. Robert DeNiro, who, in my opinion, is most probably one of the finest actors of our time.

July 9, 1990

I t all started when Deputy Fire Commissioner Bill Alletto called
and said Robert DeNiro was going to be at his City hall office,
and he wanted me to be there to meet him at 9:00 A.M.
At 8:30 A.M., I arrived at city hall. It seemed that everyone
was excited that Mr. DeNiro was coming to see Chief Alletto
about his role as a fire investigator.

When Robert DeNiro walked in, I had to take a second look.
He had a five day growth of beard, and was wearing boat shoes
without any socks. The T-shirt he had on looked one size too
large, and his hair was in disarray, not messy, but certainly not
combed. Why I had imagined that he would be in a custom-fit-
ted suit—shaved, handsome, and as he looks in the movies—I
don't know.

My first encounter with Bob was a quick handshake, and his
eye contact was even quicker than the handshake. At that
moment, I sensed that he was a shy man. His surroundings were
strange, and being in the presence of Commissioners Alletto,
Orozco, Altman, Corbett, and Chief Stan Span was even stranger.
Previously, Mr. DeNiro had been hustled through city hall to
room 105, which houses fire department headquarters. He had
met more people in ten minutes than I could accurately count.

Chief Alletto told me that he was bringing Mr. DeNiro over
to OFI, which is the Chicago Fire Department's Office of Fire
Investigation, at 1401 S. Michigan. I left my car parked there, so I

1

took a ride with Chief Stan Span. I arrived after they did, and Bob was already talking with Chief Pat Burns. Chief Burns had the day all mapped out: first to the morgue, then to some fire scenes. As they were discussing the day, I was introduced to Richard Lewis, the producer of the movie *Backdraft*. Lewis was accompanying Burns and DeNiro to the site also.

They included me in their plans along with Tom Purdy, a fire investigator with OFI. So we all headed out in Pat's car, a black four door Sedan. As we traveled through the streets of Chicago, Bob was sitting in the front seat with Pat, while Mr. Lewis sat in the back with Tom Purdy and me. Pat told us some stories about the fire department's history. Granted we were not in the nicest part of town, but Bob was so overwhelmed by the stories he didn't care or notice where he was.

The first fire scene we arrived at had just occurred the night before. It was a burned out, abandoned, two-story frame building. Engine Company 54 was still there picking up their hose lines. It was a still and box alarm, and looked to be a typical arson fire in the 18th battalion. A still and box alarm fire is one requiring five engine companies, two truck companies, a squad three battalion of chiefs, one deputy district chief, one ambulance, a communication van, and an investigator from OFI. The condition of the building was atrocious. The rear porch was completely burned away. Bob looked on with much interest; to think that such destruction was done deliberately by someone.

At that moment, it was the first time I noticed that he began to play the role of Don Rimgale, the fire investigator he would be portraying in *Backdraft*.

We continued on to 59th and Halsted Streets, and then to 55th and Halsted, where I was the investigator on both scenes. He asked me about both fires, and I told him that I had had trouble with a drunk on 59th Street, and that on my way back I had discovered the fire on 55th Street.

Our next stop was 26th and California, the Cook County Criminal Court Building. I stayed outside with the car, while Purdy, Burns, and Mr. DeNiro went to meet the Cook County state's attorneys arson task force, which was led by one of the best arson prosecution attorneys in the state of Illinois, Diane Gordon.

It was then time for lunch, and we went over to Connie's Pizza on 24th and South Archer Ave. We all ate antipasto salad and Bob had eggplant.

Our venture was coming to an end, so we headed back to OFI. We arrived about 2:00 P.M., shook hands and called it a day. It was my day off anyway, so I went home.

Later that day, about 4:00 P.M., Tom Purdy called me and asked if I would like to earn some overtime that night, driving Robert DeNiro around to fires.

I replied with a professional "yes", to make it sound like I was doing it for the money, when deep down I would have done it just for the fun of it and to hang out with DeNiro.

OFI, July 9, 2000 Hours

To start the night off, Tom Purdy told me that if we had a big fire, or if we thought the fire was going to get even bigger, we were to call Ron Howard where he was staying at 33 East Elm Street, or Robert DeNiro at the Ritz Carlton, but to ask for Mr. O'Neil's room as soon as possible. We planned ahead by putting out fire clothes in 4-6-5, which is a red/black and marked fire department sedan that is used by the OFI to respond to fires. We outfitted DeNiro and Howard in what we thought they would be comfortable wearing!

Tom and I knew it was going to be a long night, so we went out to eat. Wouldn't you know it? A fire came in very soon after that.

When the fire came in, it was approximately 2300 hours. The

location was in the 10th battalion, and located at 2410 W. Cullom. As I listened to the radio, I could just hear it in battalion Chief Kugelman's voice that he had something big on his hands. When the chief arrived on the scene, he requested a still and box alarm, and said to send in an ambulance because he had "jumpers," i.e. people who had jumped out the windows. So we made the phone calls to DeNiro and Howard.

Ritz Carlton 2315 Hours

When we pulled up in front of the Ritz Carlton Hotel, we thought they would be waiting for us. We were wrong.

DeNiro and Howard were nowhere in sight. Purdy and I looked like two nitwits in the driveway of the Ritz Carlton Hotel, what with our lights flashing, the siren sounding and with the hotel not on fire—people thought we were nuts!

In a panic, Tom ran to the front of the building to see if they were there. In the meantime, I looked up the street, and saw someone running at me with a hat on his head. As he got closer, I knew it was Ron Howard. He jumped in the back seat in a hurry.

I asked, "Where's DeNiro?"

He had no comment.

So I radioed Tom on Michigan Avenue, but before I could say anything, DeNiro walks out of the hotel like he was going for an evening stroll.

I yelled, "What the fuck are ya doing? Let's go, man. We're going to a fire!"

He then too became excited at the prospect of responding to a real fire.

Responding to the fire, I was driving really defensively fast, but safe. Tom was in the back with Howard, and DeNiro was sitting in the front with me. You could tell it was a real experience for both of them.

4

Upon our arrival at the fire, Tom and I showed them how to get into their turn out gear (fire clothes). We then approached the fire and met with Chief Kugelman. He related the situation to us, informing us that the rear of the structure was fully engulfed in flames and that there were victims.

Chief Kugelman took a good look at the four of us and couldn't believe his eyes.

"Cos, what's going on? Who are these guys?" he asked.

We hastily filled him in.

After a while, we went around to the back of the structure. Water was still dripping, and Commonwealth Edison was cutting the burned-out wires off of the pole so that we could get onto the back porch. I could tell that the fire had originated on the porch on the first floor.

"Was it arson?" Bob asked right away.

I replied that it looked to me as though the fire had originated on the rear porch and had traveled into the apartment. I was able to show Bob and Ron where the fire had started and then how to start interviewing the occupants of the structure.

I took Bob over to interview the occupants. Wouldn't you know it, they all spoke Spanish.

I thought, 'oh, shit!'

I noticed one boy, about 12-years-old, who was speaking English. I grabbed him and told him that I would pay him if he helped me out.

DeNiro looked at me like I was nuts.

Then the woman who had called the fire in to 911 started talking. She said she saw the two young boys set the fire in a mattress on the back porch. Bob and I went to take a look at it, but there was only a spring from the mattress left—that was it!

People don't lie when there are serious injuries at fires. We were at the fire approximately one and one half hours. On the ride back, Bob asked questions about the fire and about the occupants. We dropped Ron Howard off at DeNiro's request.

When we arrived back at the hotel, Bob asked me if just the two of us could go out on the next run.

"Why?" I asked.

He replied that he was going to be the fire investigator in the movie, not Ron Howard, and that Howard was just asking too many questions about the fire department and not the investigating.

We ended our fire lesson at 0245 on July 10.

I woke up the next morning, took a shower, and went downstairs to check out my rig, a red sedan. When I walked around the car, who was standing there, but Bob DeNiro. He told me how much he had enjoyed last night, and said, "I can't wait to go on the next fire."

"Why are you here so early?" I asked.

He replied, "Pat Burns called about a fire somewhere on the south side."

I followed them to the fire scene which was located at 60th and Normal.

Marshall Cucci headed the fire investigation. There was a fatality on the top floor of a three story vacant brick building. The fire had occurred about four hours before our arrival. It was a minor fire, but there was a death and that made it a priority investigation.

I watched DeNiro.

He had a tape recorder with him, and it was always on. He was always asking more and more questions about if it was arson. I didn't know what he was after at that time, but I knew it was something.

Pat Burns then took Bob to the county morgue to view the burn victim's body. I didn't go with them because I had other duties to attend to.

That whole day I couldn't stop thinking about DeNiro and how interested in fire investigation he was. I called Deputy Fire

Commissioner Alletto to tell him how much I was enjoying being with DeNiro, and he explained some "do's and don'ts" about fire investigation and responding. I also told him how interested DeNiro was in fire investigation and Chief Alletto was pleased.

"Stay with him," he said. "Start taking notes."

That night, at about 2100 hours, I placed a call to Bob to see how he felt. He was glad to hear from me.

He asked me some questions about the fire that had happened last night and about the fatality. He told me that the morgue was interesting but he didn't think he needed to see that again. He had found out the guy did not die as a result of the fire. He had been murdered, hit by a blunt object on the back of his neck!

I asked him how he felt, and if he wanted to go out that night if there were any fires.

He replied, "Yes," that if I thought it was a fire he should see, he wanted to go. He told me he was exhausted from last night and all day today and that he was going to get some sleep.

July 11, 1990, 0400

I was awakened by the main fire alarm office and told to respond to a 2-11 alarm fire at 3829 North Oakley. A 2-11 alarm fire is where approximately 25 pieces of fire equipment respond, along with about 100 fire personnel.

Our presence had been requested by 5th battalion Chief Dwyer.

I called Bob and told him we had an extra alarm fire in a warehouse on the north side, and he asked me how soon I would be there.

"Five minutes," I said.

He said he would be waiting and, sure enough, he was.

I picked him up at the Ritz Carlton Hotel and we responded to the fire...all the time the fire radio in the car was giving out orders for fire companies responding to the fire. I was trying to explain to him what they were about. DeNiro had his tape recorder on the whole time.

When we arrived on the scene of the 2-11 alarm, he asked me to tell him about each procedure I was performing, while I was doing it.

First, I told him to put his boots on. "I can get an exterior look around the fire scene," I said.

Second, I told him to take the fire coat out of the car and stand away while he put it on. "Keep on looking around," I said. "Now button the coat as you walk back up to the car."

Third, I put on my truckman's belt as I still looked around.

Bob asked why I didn't carry the hand light instead of having it hooked on the truckman's belt.

"I always have to have the use of my two hands. This way, I always have my light immediately available." I said.

The fourth move I made was to put my handi-talkie radio in my fire coat, along with my notebook and my fire helmet. I explained that it was important to lock up the car and put the keys in your pockets.

"Why?" Bob asked.

"So when you come back to the car, it will still be there!"

Bob looked at me and said with a smile, "Good idea."

As we approached the fire, I was nervous and quite sure that he was too. I met with 2-1-14, Chief Crane, who at the time was the district incident commander, to ask him some questions about the fire. I told him that I was helping Robert DeNiro with his part in the movie, *Backdraft*."

"Have a good time," Chief Crane said, as we walked around to the front of the building. "I have a fire to put out."

I explained to DeNiro why aerial trucks were placed here and pumpers there, and that such placement had a strategic tactical purpose.

Bill Cosgrove

"Now let's take a look inside the building," I said.

I thought he would balk at going in, but no, he went right in. It was very smoky, and we stayed low and followed the lines up to where the firefighters were working. There was a lot of fire, and a part of the roof caved in. Bob asked me if it was safe inside the building.

I said, "If they are in here with the fire hose I feel safe."

He just shrugged and calmly said, "OK".

We were just getting in the way of extinguishment at this time, so we backed out and found that there was a drinking fountain in the smoke-filled room.

"Would you like a drink?" I asked.

He looked at me with that DeNiro grin, and I knew he liked it, the idea of taking a drink of ice cold Lake Michigan water in a fire building. We looked at each other and both of us laughed at the irony of it.

We walked around the structure. A Chicago Fire Department photographer took our picture.

"Who was that?" Bob asked.

"Howard Zelinka," I replied.

We approached the loading dock at the rear of the burning structure, and we walked into water that was about 18 inches deep. He looked up with another one of those looks that he gives, but I told him, "Don't worry."

Again he just smiled and moved along slowly into the deep water.

We climbed a straight ladder, about four feet up, on the dock platform where the fire companies were working with handlines.

I talked to Chief Dwyer of the 5th battalion. There was fire issuing about 20 feet over the roof of the building. There were firemen cutting open an overhead door to get in to the fire with handlines. Bob was in awe of their dedication, competence and determination.

We climbed back down again into the water and made our

9

way to the outside of the building. Bob told me his foot was hurting but that he could keep going.

We talked with the owner of the structure and a Chicago police officer, and also with the woman that had notified the fire department, the person who had discovered the fire. Robert DeNiro asked the woman where she first saw the flames.

By this time Bob was limping. I told him, "We have to take a look at your foot."

It was raining, now and we found the front porch of a Chicago bungalow. I pulled his fire boot off and, sure thing, there was a reddened blister on the side of his foot.

"Where are your socks?" I asked.

He told me he doesn't wear socks!

"When you wear fire boots, *you wear socks!*" I informed him. I took my socks off and gave them to Bob to wear on his feet and we continued with the investigation.

We made our way back into the structure and by now the smoke had lifted considerably. On the one side of the building the roof was gone and we went to see if we could determine how heavily damaged this section of the roof was. The fire had originated in this section we learned, based on the information we received from Chief Dwyer, who explained that upon arrival of the initial response companies, the fire had been issuing from the roof at the rear of the building. We found a boiler located in this section, and after asking the owner about it, he stated that it was to be turned on one hour before the people went to work. After a thorough fire scene investigation, we determined that the fire had been accidental in origin, and was the result of malfunction of the subject boiler.

We returned to the OFI fire car and, as we approached, I met a fireman from the fire department repair shops, Frank Leberis, who was driving the fuel truck. I introduced him to Mr. DeNiro, and asked him to stay by the OFI car while I got my information for 2-7-1, the communications van. As we were leaving the fire scene, Bob said what a funny guy Frank was and as we drove away we both started to laugh. It was that time of morning when the birds start chirping and night blends into day.

As we drove back to the hotel, Bob asked about the fire and if we could get a cup of coffee. There was a White Castle down the street, which serves some of the best coffee in Chicago. We drank the coffee in the car in the parking lot, and engaged in small talk about how many years I'd been on the job, kids, wife, etc. He asked me why I didn't ask him for his autograph.

I said, "I don't know why. Maybe because you didn't ask me for mine."

He looked at me with that DeNiro look and started to laugh.

The ice was broken, and it seemed that, from that moment on, we were completely at ease with each other. The camaraderie that had begun during the fire, rain, and the exchanging of socks had now become cemented. He asked me if I was interested in advising him and taking him to more fires.

"That's beyond my control," I explained, "I work the first shift and I'm off duty now. If you want to go to a fire, then you have to go with someone from the second shift."

He didn't seem sold on that. "Would you like to help me research my part and take me to fires?" he asked.

"Yeah, sure, but you'll have to talk to the chief and arrange it with him."

"Don't worry, I'll take care of everything. I'll talk to Ron."

The fire station at 14th and Michigan is at most ten minutes from the Ritz. I knew something was up when I pulled up and the big overhead door opened automatically. Usually, I have to open the door myself.

About ten guys were standing around with inquisitive looks on their faces as I backed the fire car into the firehouse.

Chief Burns was standing by his office door and barked at

Robert DeNiro (right) and the author at a fire scene
on the north side of Chicago.

me. "Where the hell have you been?" he asked.

"I went to a 2-11 with DeNiro."

"Well, what did you tell him?"

"We just went through the steps that we do as fire investigators."

"Yeah," the chief continued, "but you should have been back a long time ago."

"We stopped for some coffee because we were cold and wet. Then I took him back to his hotel."

"Well, we have been getting a lot of calls, and Chief Span is on his way over to talk to you."

I went and had a cup of coffee, and by the time I got back

Chief Span was already there. With a serious look on his face, he asked me directly, "What we need to know is, what did you tell DeNiro?"

"I told him a lot of things."

"No," he interjected. "You told him something about how you were going to work with him?"

I felt a little uncomfortable, as though I was being interrogated. "I never said I was going to work with him," I said. "He asked me if I could and I told him today was my day off."

Chief Span said, "Well, whether you know it or not, you are his technical advisor. Ron Howard was called by DeNiro and he has requested you."

"It had taken Bob only about ten minutes to get through the chain of command. To do something like this normally would have taken two weeks. I was now given some ground rules to follow.

First of all, Robert DeNiro was not allowed to ride in any city vehicles.

Second, when we responded to any fires, I was prohibited from using flashing lights or the siren.

The next thing to figure out was how I would be able to work on the movie without it interfering with my job. Chief Alletto said to run my two furloughs together, and then we would see how much more time I would need.

I returned home and, at approximately 11:00 A.M., Bob DeNiro called and asked if everything was all set for me to advise him technically on the movie.

I told him I would be more than happy to work with him.

Bob told me that the first thing he wanted me to do was to go over some things that were in the script, and he asked if I could come to the Ritz Carlton Hotel later on that day. He then gave me a number for the production office in order to have a way to reach him.

I then called the Chicago Production Office, 5660 W. Taylor, to find out how I was to obtain the OFI car. I talked to Alecia La Rue and she said that she had been waiting for my call and wanted to meet the person who had been picked by DeNiro to be his technical advisor.

I arrived at the production office at about 7:00 P.M. I met with Alecia and she introduced me to George DeLeonardi, the transportation coordinator, and he showed me a company car, which looked exactly like our OFI cars. Mr. DeLeonardi gave me an identification card for gas and to get the car washed. He wished me good luck and I put my fire gear in the car.

I returned to the office and told Alecia that I had to go to wardrobe to pick out some fire gear for Mr. DeNiro. She introduced me to Cheryl Webber who had five fire coats for me to pick from and boots and a helmet. I could not believe that he was that important. They said Mr. DeWaay said, "Anything that Bill Cosgrove needs, get it for him." (Who is DeWaay? He signs the checks.)

At approximately 8:30 P.M. I left the production office, and was traveling east on the Eisenhower Expressway, thinking to myself about how this had all happened. The fire radio was blaring, and now I was listening to every word to see if there was a hit. A hit is the fireman's term for a working fire, and if there was one in the city, we were going.

I arrived at the Ritz Carlton Hotel and, once inside, was asked what I was there for. I never thought about the fact that I had a fire car outside and that I was in my uniform.

I informed the doorman that I was there to see Mr. DeNiro.

He called someone who said, "Send him up."

I was escorted to the 24th floor of the Ritz Carlton and to the suite of one of the most famous actors in the country. I knocked on his door. When he opened it, he said, "Come on in, Bill."

We shook hands and he thanked me for coming. He was very concerned that I was out late at night just to help him. He didn't

Robert DeNiro (far right) and the author interviewing the owner
of this structure and a Chicago Police Officer.

---

know how excited I was to be there. He offered me a beer.

I answered, "If you're having one."

The apartment was plush, the 24th floor, overlooking Lake
Michigan. We sat at the dining room table, and Bob told me that
Pat was a nice guy and so was Rimgale, but he had not come here
to learn about the history of the Chicago Fire Department. He
had to learn how to conduct the proper investigations of the different types of fires that occurred in the movie script and scenes.

So we opened the script and started to figure out the theory
of a trychtichlorate and fires in electrical outlets. As we talked, I
started to see how intent he was to learn what I knew about fire
investigation, as he listened to every word, watching me express
myself. After a couple of beers, we started to be more relaxed in

15

each other's company. He asked me about the fire department and how I became a fireman.

I told him about my late father who was a fireman and my brothers, and—the best of all—about my mother. I told him about my wife, Suzi, and my six children, and how I had joined my father and my brother in becoming a fireman; how my mother had raised ten children on $145.00 per month, and how she would listen to the fire radio that she kept on her night stand. Firefighting was in our family's blood, but the price to pay for such a profession was often steep. My father had died at the age of 46, and my brother, Jim, died at the age of 51. Though neither were killed directly by fire, they had succumbed to the various side effects associated with long-term smoke inhalation.

I asked Bob if he wanted to listen for some fires. We would need a portable fire radio. We talked about other things that we would need to make responding to fires a little easier.

It was getting late so I got ready to leave.

He said, "If there is a fire in Chicago tonight, call me."

I told him "10-4."

He liked that.

I got into the car. It was 0025. I got a sandwich from a deli on 8th and State Street. I sat around for about one hour and ate my sandwich. The radio was silent and I then went home to get some sleep.

Sunday morning, about 1000, Bob called and said that he had called DeWaay about the portable fire radio and that we would have it tomorrow at the set, which was at Pat O'Sullivans Pub, located at 495 N. Milwaukee. The set call time was scheduled for 7:00 P.M.

I went to the production office at 5:00 P.M. and exchanged my fire gear, then got the red sedan, and they told me to meet DeNiro at the set.

Bill Cosgrove

People were all around. Campers, trailers, and semi-trailers were all over the place. I asked someone where to meet Robert DeNiro and the guy just looked at me like, are you nuts? I parked the car and started looking around for someone that I knew. I read the script but did not understand why the movie was starting here. DeNiro wasn't in this part.

Now I entered the pub, waiting for someone to talk to me but no one did. The interior of the pub was decked out with fire memorabilia, pictures, helmets, boots, and pike poles, also fire axes and trophies. You name it and it was in there. Most of the things were borrowed from the Gaelic Fire Brigade.

I looked out the window and saw Ron Howard. I knew that he knew who I was, because of the ride in the OFI car and the fire I had taken him to the other night on Cullum. Ron greeted me as though he had known me all his life and graciously thanked me for the great job of taking him and Bob to the fire the other night. He also told me where Robert DeNiro's trailer was parked.

When I saw Bob, he was just pulling up in a white Cadillac. He got out and came over to me, and thanked me for showing up and said that the portable radio was in his trailer. As we walked to his trailer, we small talked. He asked me if I had everything I needed, and if not, that we would get it.

Inside his trailer, I met Robert DeNiro's make-up and hair stylist, Ilona Herman. She appeared to be a quiet person; good looking, ageless, blond. I did not know what to say to her or to him.

DeNiro gave me the radio and said that if a fire came in and I thought we should go to it, that we'd be gone. In the meantime, however, he had to get ready to take pictures.

I waited outside and walked around for a while. When a young man came to me and said, "Mr. DeNiro would like to see you." I ran to his trailer like it was an emergency.

17

Once inside, he said, "How do I look?"

He had a white fire uniform shirt on with blue pants, and he was now shaved clean but he had a mustache like mine.

I was in awe. His hair was parted down the middle, and with the mustache he looked just like me.

"You look great," I told him.

Ilona said she did not like the mustache. Bob explained to me that if he walked out onto the set and they took pictures, that would be that. He called Ron and Rich Lewis in, and they all agreed: no mustache.

I then went up to the set and Bob was driven up in the white car. The people crowded around as he got out. There was a rumble in the crowd: "That's him."

I stood across the street and watched. Ron Howard came to his side. They talked for a second. I then knew that he was the most important person in the movie.

I had met his driver, Todd, on the first day at OFI headquarters. As he looked across the street, Todd noticed me and gave a hand signal to come over.

I looked at him, as if to say, "Who, me?"

Todd told Bob, "Cos is over there."

DeNiro looked over and said, "Come on over here."

I had thought that side was for the movie people only. Well, I was a movie person from that time on, and as I came around the white car, and Bob and Ron approached me, Bob said, "No mustache. Do you think I still look alright?"

I could not answer right away, because I was choking to myself without making a sound and because Bob looked so different now, clean-shaven.

Ilona said, "Billy, Bob wants you by his side at all times when he's on the set." She had this certain way of saying things, and you knew that it was important to pay attention.

Bob pulled me over and said, "From now on, you are my

technical advisor." He added, "Even though I am not in this part of the movie, I still have to be on the set for still pictures."

I looked around at the crowd. There were hundreds of people and I knew they were looking at the stars but I thought they were all looking at me...Ha, Ha!

At that time, a fellow brought a cup of what I thought was coffee but it was cappuccino. Bob looked at me and said, "Cos, you want some cappuccino?"

I had no idea what the hell it was but I said, "Sure, I would love a cup."

Bob had to try on fire helmets, coats and boots. Then they would take his picture and he would say, "How do they look on me?"

I told him, "No, they don't look too good. You are too clean looking. Fire gear has to be salty looking, washed out looking, like you went to a lot of fires."

Bob asked me to get my fire coat. As I did, Ron Howard said, "Where is your coat?"

I told him, "In the fire car, 4-6-8 on the next block."

He told one of the assistants to get the car up here. They did. With my portable radio in my back pocket and my fire coat on the hood of the car, DeNiro told a wardrobe lady, "That's the fire coat I want."

I pulled my radio out of my pocket. While I was listening to a still and box, Bob came over and asked, "Do we have something?"

I told him that Engine 57 had just pulled up to a scene and had reported a working fire.

Someone said to DeNiro, "You're not going to a fire."

But DeNiro answered, "If Cos says we go, we go."

They—his people—just did not know what to say.

We went back to the trailer and Bob changed into a new outfit, some dry clothes. The dry clothes consisted of a regular shirt and pants, no uniform, and we returned to the set for more pictures.

Bob left at 11 P.M., but I stayed for about an hour to watch what was going on. I got home at about 1:00 A.M. Suzi, my wife, was waiting to hear about all the things I did, so we stayed up half the night talking about this new movie-making experience.

The red sedan fire car marked 4-6-8, OFI, was delivered to my house. I was on the set by 6:00 P.M. DeNiro wasn't there yet, but now people were coming up to me, asking how I was picked to be his technical advisor and I told them I didn't know. I later found out that Deputy Fire Commissioner Alletto had arranged it through Fire Commissioner Orozco and 1st Deputy Fire Commissioner Altman.

Soon the white Cadillac came around the corner. Everyone knew that DeNiro was here. When he got out, he came right over to the OFI car, and he asked me how I was doing and made other small talk. We looked in the trunk. All his gear was there and he asked me if I had my personal copy of the script with me.

Then we went into the trailer and, while Ilona was doing his hair, we talked about him and his character, Don Rimgale. He told me that like the other characters in the movie, to be played by William Baldwin and Kurt Russell, he was a loner—no history or family. He also stated that he had saved Ronald from a certain death (Ronald was a bad guy, a psychotic arsonist). But in the process, he had been badly burned, and the fire had left his shadow on the wall. This is how he got the nickname "Shadow." Bob asked me if I knew anyone who had been burned badly, because in the movie make-up gave his character scars that he sustained at the fire where he saved Ronald.

Bob finished up what he had to do. I was outside with Ilona and Todd Dickinson, Bob's driver, and was told that DeNiro wanted to see "Cos." I went into the trailer and Mr. DeNiro asked me if I wanted to go over the script with him that night.

We left the set in the red sedan. On the way out, we were stopped by an off-duty Chicago police officer named O'Meara, who was assigned to the bomb and arson section. We made small talk and then left.

Mr. DeNiro said he heard about some streets under downtown Chicago that were lit up in green lights (lower Wacker Drive). We went up Milwaukee, over to Lake Street, and east to Wacker Drive. We talked about some history of Chicago as he viewed lower Wacker Drive. He thought it was neat. Bob asked me if he could drive the fire car, and I said sure, but he did not want to drive it that night.

We drove around talking about fire investigation, mainly arson and arsonists, but all that time I wasn't sure of what he was after regarding fire cause investigation. It was about midnight. As we drove around downtown Chicago, I related to Bob that we call this area of the city "the loop."

Bob asked about this guy who was an arsonist that Ron Howard had told him about.

"You mean 'Fat Albert'," I said. "Yes, we have a guy that was suspect in the deliberate setting of fires. The police and OFI finally got enough evidence to put him behind bars. His name was Albert Zenner and in 1977 he was convicted of arson and got three to seven years for it. He did about three and one half years."

Bob asked if he could meet this guy, saying that it would help in developing the character that he was playing in the movie.

"I'll check with some people, but I don't think they'll approve," I said.

I called Tony Maritato, a fireman who was in OFI with me and he said, "No problem," that he would set it up.

Bob asked me to go over what an investigator does from the time he first receives the alarm. We were getting tired of driving around, so I said, "Let's stop somewhere," not knowing how he felt.

He said, "Where can we go that's not too crowded?"

I realized that he didn't want to be noticed. I told him that I always go to the filtration plant or to the planetarium to finish a fire investigation job, because it was quiet and we could think.

He enthusiastically said, "Let's go."

We set out on Lake Shore Drive, heading south. We went around Soldier Field and down Planetarium Drive. There were a lot of cars parked around. We drove down by Megs Field, and Bob loved the view of the downtown Chicago skyscape. I told him that there were places I would go to sort out my fire facts, the who, what, and where of fires by myself. We drove around the planetarium and back on Lake Shore Drive.

Listening to the radio, I took him to the 31st Street Beach. It was too crowded.

It was easy to talk to him now, much easier. The more he told me about the character he would play, the more I started to understand.

We went to the filtration plant, the ultimate place. Nobody was there. When we entered the gate a policeman passed us through because we were in a fire car. It was a long drive in past the fire boat, Engine 37, and out where only the filtration employees work.

I placed the red sedan facing out, because it was a dead end. If anyone came along, we could pull out of a dead end and he, Bob, would not be seen.

"Never pull into somewhere you can't pull out of," I said.

Bob liked that saying. I told him that an old friend of mine, fire Captain Matt Moran, had told me that.

We got out of the car and stretched our legs. I pointed out that his apartment was right there at the Ritz Carlton. If we did not get a run and he got tired, he would be home in two minutes. It was beautiful out that evening and the city skyscape was breathtaking! The stars were shining and the sky was clear. The temperature was about 70 degrees, and you could hear the waves from Lake Michigan splashing against the rocks on shore...it was perfect!

We took the script out. We started where his part began in the movie. We took both scripts, his and mine, and put them on the hood of the car on page 14, scene #24 which introduced Rimgale:

Exterior Brownstone

Rimgale lights cigarette, slowly looks around, puts on his fire boots and helmet, then gets his tools.

We practiced sitting in the car, then getting our boots, coat and helmet on and off about one hundred times. Mr. DeNiro asked about no less than one thousand times what my actions were when I got out of the car. We put our boots on, we put our fire coats on...ten different ways.

We lit cigarettes. We leaned against the car.

The man was truly motivated about his part in the movie.

We laughed and made small talk. When we called it a night at 4:00 A.M., I took him back to the Ritz Carlton Hotel.

The next morning, Mr. DeNiro called to see how I was feeling. He was concerned more about me than I was for myself. We talked about the night before and how much work had been accomplished.

He thought it was work.

He talked to Brad, my youngest son, making small talk. Then he told me that set call was at 6:00 P.M., but that he had make-up and hair at 5:00 P.M.

I wasn't sure about what he meant.

Bob explained that everyday we would get a call sheet, and that he would have to be at the movie set to get ready about an hour before starting work.

Forty-second & Drexel Boulevard was one of the locations that I had found with Mike Malone, the location manager, back in April. I parked the red sedan at the corner, in between the boulevard center median strip. When I looked at the buildings, I could not believe my eyes. What had been two abandoned buildings before, were now two lovely brownstones with landscaped new lawns, glass in the windows, light fixtures, and curtains in the windows. It looked just great! This was my old fire district, and previously it had a great many burned-out buildings.

I met Ron Howard. He was so nice to me, thanking me for doing such a good job with DeNiro. He said that if I needed anything, to call Alecia LaRue and I would get it. Then I was escorted to Mr. DeNiro's trailer.

Bob wasn't on the set, so I looked around. From up the street came the white "caddie." Bob got out and came right over to me. He embraced me with a hug and asked me how I was doing as we went into the trailer. Inside, Ilona was moving stuff around, putting things in the fridge.

Bob had some questions on his mind about the script. We went over them.

He changed into the clothes he was to wear on the set, blue pants, white striped shirt and navy shoes. With each item he put on, he asked me about how it looked, and if this was the type of clothes he should have on. Then we looked at the shoes. Navy issue. He did not like them; he wanted wing tips like I was wearing.

To my surprise, in comes a girl with a pair of wing tips just like mine. That's when I started to understand that he was trying to be just like me in looks and actions.

We left the trailer and went up to the set, and they set the main camera on Mr. DeNiro. They took side shots, front shots, and back shots. Then we went inside to see the set that would be used. We looked around at the propane tanks and the cannons at the front door.

Ron was telling us what was going to happen to the first victim, Alan Seagrave, in the fire that night. We went around the back to see. That part of the building was still the ghetto.

Bob looked at me and said, "How long did you work on Truck 15 in this shit?"

I answered, "Too long, twelve and one half years."

We went over to Craft Service where this guy had all this food and coffee and drinks. We had more coffee. The Craft Service guy was Ray Bulinski.

My old pal from OFI, Tony Maritato, came to the movie set, and told me that he had it all arranged for DeNiro to meet "Fat Albert" on July 28th.

We talked to Bob and he said that Ron Howard also wanted to meet him. Tony Maritato told us to meet him in the back of the fire department shops, at the place where one of the old fire boats was in the Chicago River.

Bob told Ron Howard and he said that would be fine with him.

Tony told Deputy Fire Commissioner Alletto that we had this meeting set up. He said that before any such meeting, he wanted to see what the fire commissioner had to say about it, since Chief Alletto did not feel this was a good thing to do.

Commissioner Orozco said, "Absolutely NO!" He did not want this guy to have any credit for being an arsonist, because he might start setting fires again. "No way!"

Deputy Commissioner Alletto agreed with the Boss's decision, because he didn't like it either!

Back in the trailer, Bob and I drank our coffee. Ilona was working with a Polaroid camera taking pictures of Bob. Then they went in the other room, which was a bedroom with a dressing table.

Bob called me in and told me that Ilona was going to fix his hair and make-up, because according to the script it was late at night.

Then we got called to the fire for "Mr. Seagrave", which was the scene where the guy gets blown off of the porch and into the windshield of his car. We went out to see the first shot, in which Seagrave entered the brownstone. He walked up to the front door.

Bob was standing next to me, behind a plexiglass partition. We looked at each other when Ron Howard said, "And action."

There was a flash and boom, and Mr. Seagrave landed on the ground in front of the car. Bob looked at me with awe. This was very dangerous.

We then left the set and went back to the trailer. Bob told Ilona that we were going to do some work and listen to the portable fire radio.

We got into the red sedan and headed for Lake Shore Drive. We talked about the blast and how dangerous it was, and also about other movies he had been in that were dangerous, like the movie *Deerhunter*, where in a scene in the River Kwa they were being rescued by a helicopter, he and John Savage, and one of the runners caught a cable on the bridge.

"We let go and flopped into the water. I thought the helicopter was going to fall on us. It was a very bad scene, but we were able to swim to shore," he said.

Mr. DeNiro told me about another scene that was dangerous in *Deerhunter*. It was a car scene where they were driving up the mountain to hunt in this caddie. They had cameras mounted on the side of the car and were being towed by a film crew. There was a cliff wall on the left side of the car and they were traveling fast. They kept getting close to the wall and one time hit the rocks. One of the cameras broke loose and almost came through the windshield. Bob had to put his arms up to cover his face. Talk about a close call!

As we approached the filtration plant, we talked about fires. You could tell that arson was on his mind. He so much wanted to respond to a fire that was arson.

It was a perfect night. The lake was calm as we opened the tool box to familiarize Bob with the investigative tools that we used in OFI. There was a lot of action on the radio, and we listened to a fire at 124 N. Halsted.

The still alarm (first engine in) was Engine 5, and we heard the officer in charge say, "Emergency, give us a box." That's a saying for a still and box. I looked at DeNiro and said, "That's a hit. Let's go."

Although we were not supposed to use the emergency light and siren, we did anyway. We got there right away.

It was a one story brick building and fire was issuing through the roof. I told Bob to get his fire gear on, and since this was just a still and box, that we could take our time until the firemen got in and knocked it down. We came down an alley to the rear so as not to be noticed.

The fire was almost out and well under control when we entered the rear door. The third platoon was working so I did not know too many of the firemen. (I always worked the first platoon).

We looked around to find the point of the fire's origin, which turned out to be a workbench in the center of the structure. Then we interviewed a worker who stated that all of the lights in the place had dimmed on and off two or three times. He had walked into the workshop, only to see fire and a lot of arcing on this workbench. Bob was disappointed that it wasn't an arson fire.

We went back to the sedan, took off our turn-out gear, and started to get into the car. Looking at him over the roof of the car, I asked, "Do you want to call it a night?"

As always, he responded, "How do you feel?"

I said that I felt good.

Then he asked me, "Would you mind going over a few more things?"

I said fine.

We stopped for a coffee to go at a donut shop and went back to the filtration plant. Bob told me he felt good about this place.

The filtration plant was a beautiful spot on the Michigan lake-front.

We started with the tools again, then the fire clothes and the donning of the helmet. I said to myself, "This guy is a perfectionist!"

All of a sudden, there was a loud noise, and Bob asked, "What was that?"

"What?"

Bob said, "Over there, by the rocks by the lake."

We started walking toward the rocks, when all of a sudden two big birds—I'm not sure what type they were, but they were big—jumped out and flew away. We kind of grabbed each other's arms, not wanting to admit that we were really spooked. We laughed about it all night, till 4:00 A.M.

Thursday, July 19

The next morning, Mr. DeNiro called about 11:30 A.M.

"How are you?" I asked.

We laughed more about the birds. Then we talked about the work that we would do that night. He asked me to meet him at the set, to go over the script outside the building. He told me that his make-up and hair time was 6:00 P.M. and set call was at 7:00 P.M.

I arrived at 5:30 P.M., and parked the sedan in the same place. Ron Howard was in front of the building, so I walked down to where he was standing and noticed that they had put poor "Mr. Seagrave" in the windshield. It looked real.

Ron Howard said, "We need the red sedan in the shot." Then he asked, "How are you and Bob getting along?"

I told him about the fire the night before and he was interested to see if it was an arson.

I looked around for the white caddie. Robert DeNiro had not yet arrived on the set.

I went to the trailer and Ilona was busy working. She said to me, "Bob just loves you. He told me you worked all night and went to a big fire."

She called him on the car phone. He was ten minutes away.

Sure enough, about ten minutes later, the white caddie pulled up and there was a rumble among the crew and spectators.

"DeNiro's here!"

Bob got out and came right over to me.

"How do you feel today?" he asked. "Good, I hope."

We walked to the trailer.

There was a problem with his fire coat: it was too "salty." Jodie, the costume designer, said it didn't look good on film. About ten coats later they found one that was just perfect.

We went over how he would approach the car, look at the fire victim, and then look at the crowd with no surprise on his face, in order to give the impression that he was a tough old professional, a "salty" fireman—which he sure did.

The scene did not even faze him. He got out of the car, looked at the building, the crowd of people. He turned back to the car. Put on the helmet, lit a smoke, looked at the crowd, then the building. He approached the car, looked at victim, then the crowd with no surprise on his face. He was a salty fireman. Over and over again, we went through the scene.

Suzi came over. She met Bob and there was small talk. He was so precise and exact about his part. He grew quiet then and he seemed a little uptight.

I left for a while to let him be alone. By that point, I had gotten to know his moods, and could tell that he was now in a "state of contemplation." He wanted to be just perfect in every detail!

The movie people called Bob to the set. The door opened and Ilona said to me, "Now stay with Bob," and we walked up the set and met with Ron Howard.

Ron wanted to show us the next scene, the one where Kurt would ask Bob about the cause of the fire. I had asked Bob if there was a chance to put a line in here for an old fireman friend who passed away, Norman Doolan. Whenever we came out of a fire building—Norm was the chief's driver—and we would ask him what was the cause of the fire, Norm would say, "Mice with matches."

Robert DeNiro asked Ron Howard and Ron said, "Sure," that it was a great line, "because we don't want anyone to know the exact cause just yet." We went into the brownstone, and to my surprise it looked just like a real fire scene.

Ron Howard was asking me how we could get a shot at a certain angle of Bob working when Kurt asks him the question. Together we figured out where to put the tools and flashlight, so that Bob would then be observing the charring on a door jamb. When Kurt Russell walked in and asks, "Shadow, you got a cause?" DeNiro would retort with his "mice with matches" line.

It was about a half hour later, when we came outside and found Fire Commissioner Ray Orozco standing in front. He asked me if I would introduce his wife, Pat, to Robert DeNiro, Kurt Russell and Ron Howard.

Suzi was watching from across the street as we walked back to the trailer. She could not believe I was with all these people. My wife was very impressed!

I left Bob for a while, and had a coke with Suzi until they called Bob again up to the set. He was real quiet now, as we went by the red sedan parked in front of the brownstone.

They started to yell, "Quiet on the set!"

I backed away and then the background smoke started to issue and Ron Howard said, "ACTION."

We did this take ten times. With smoke in the air, Robert DeNiro makes his first appearance in the movie *Backdraft*, and he was great, really believable, just like many of the old pros that we, in the fire service, knew through the years. He did this take about seven times, then we walked back to his trailer.

A 2-11 alarm had been sounded on the west side, and I told Bob.

He said, "let's go," since he was a wrap for today. As we were responding to the fire incident, I had the lights and siren on, and told him how good the first scene was that he had just shot.

We arrived at the fire scene in approximately 20 minutes. Bob and I put on our fire turn-out gear, locked up the car and proceeded to the fire scene.

The building involved was a three story brick one with a courtway, and the fire was on the second floor. There were two people injured who had already been removed by ambulance.

We entered the building and went right to the second floor. The area of origin had been a sofa bed in the rear apartment.

We met Chief Bedore of the 13th battalion and he said, "Hey, Cos, you're not on the third shift. What are you doing here?"

I pulled him to the side and told him what we were doing and introduced him to Bob.

He said that a little girl had been burned and removed to St. Mary of Nazareth Hospital. As we were walking out of the building, there were T.V. news cameras in front. Bob told me to take the lead and he was right behind me.

As we got close to the street, Bob said, "I think they noticed me."

With that, one of the firemen said, "Hey, that's DeNiro."

We looked at each other and both said, "Let's get out of here."

Back at the sedan, I asked, "Do you want to go to the hospital?"

Bob responded, "If this was your fire, would you go?"

"Yes."

He said, "Let's go."

We drove over to St. Mary of Nazareth Hospital at 1120 North

Leavitt, and as we entered the parking lot, I looked at Bob and saw that he had on a white T-shirt. We had to trade shirts. He took the fire shirt and I put on his white T-shirt, with my badge hanging off the collar.

We went into the emergency room. There were two cops there from the fire, and they said that the little girl was being worked on. We met some doctors and nurses, and told them that we were fire investigators and asked if we could talk to the little girl to see if she could tell us anything about the fire and how it got started. They said it would be alright and, as we approached the side of the bed, I told the little girl that we were firemen. Bob was next to me. She was burned on her hands and arms.

"Does it hurt?" I asked.

She said yes.

"Can I see the burns? How did the fire start?"

She told me that she had been playing with matches while her grandfather was caring for her.

Bob put his hand on the side of the bed and told the little girl it would be alright. I saw the compassion and true feelings on his face and in his eyes...I said to myself, 'This is an alright guy!'

When we were on our way out, the doctor told us that the grandfather had passed away as a result of the fire. I went in and got the name from the police. Bob was very quiet as we left.

Back at the Ritz Carlton Hotel, Bob was beat and so was I. He asked me if I could come up about noon the next day and I said O.K. When I got home it was about 3:30 A.M.

Bob called me at about 10:00 A.M., and asked me how I felt. We talked about the fire and the little girl. He was very concerned about how she was doing. We talked about fires in outlets, and I told him that I had some electrical things to show him and that I would bring them with me that day.

He asked me if I could come over and pick him up, and said

that we were going to meet Ron at the Uptown Theater to go over the next scene at 1:00 P.M.

I parked the sedan outside the Ritz and went in.

Bob met me at the door of his suite. The suite was deluxe, with a living room and dining room, and had windows facing the lake. I pointed to the easterly direction and said, "That's the filtration plant where we work on the script at night."

We sat at a table in the dining room and went over some parts in the script. He ordered coffee. As we drank our coffee we saw that all of the fires in the script originated in duplex outlets. I had brought two or three 1900 boxes and duplex outlets. We went over them, and he said it helped him understand what he was acting and saying in the movie.

Bob got ready and we left the Ritz. We drove north on Lake Shore Drive. The whole time he was talking about arson and fire. I never thought that an actor could be that interested in fire investigation.

The Uptown Theater was an old, famous, and now abandoned theater, all boarded up in the front. I asked a guy how to get in.

He said to go around the back. We did.

I said to Bob, "You in the back door: Ha, Ha."

Bob and I walked down the aisles which seemed to go on forever. As we went down the aisle, we saw there were four guys off to the side, Ron Howard, Rich Lewis, Larry DeWaay and Ian Wolf. They greeted Bob and I, and then they started talking business, so I just started looking around.

There were two lights that were shining on a doorway, and as I approached that doorway I could see a nameplate. The closer I got, the more the name looked like "COSGROVE". ...and it was!

There was a big laugh and loud clapping. Bob was in on the joke: the name on the door was supposed to be "Benton." They all came over to me and said that they hoped I wasn't mad. Ron said, "The name Benton was too plain, so we used yours."

Larry DeWaay said, "You get extra pay for the use of your name: 100 and no/100."

We laughed, and I said, "Sure it's OK, but I understand this guy gets killed."

We all laughed.

Ron started off by opening the doors to "Donald Cosgrove's" office, trying to explain what he wanted to occur during the next scene. The room was recreated to be an office in the backstage area of the structure that had just had a fire.

Ron Howard explained that Bob DeNiro's character was holding his tape recorder and was searching for some signs or indicators to show where the fire originated. The set was created by Designer Albert Brenner and I actually thought there had been a fire in the room. That was how good it was created.

Bob came over to me and said, "This is where I say 'you sneaky son of a bitch, hide and seek...come on, tell me what I want to know'. What are some indicators?"

I scratched my head. I remembered that a light bulb, an unbroken light bulb, exposed to approximately 900 degrees F. for sixty minutes tends to distend toward the heat source. I went out to the car to get one of my fire investigation books, so that I could show them what an unbroken bulb looks like after a fire is extinguished.

Bob said, "Good idea."

They put a light in back of the room and Al Brenner had a light bulb made just like the one I showed him in the book.

Next we went toward the stairs that led up the hallway. Ron asked me if we could have dead rats in the hallway and if I had ever seen them at a fire scene.

I said, "Rats are good in this scene because of the vacant building."

Then we came up to a room off the hall. The windows were broken and there was a demarcation line. There was a v-pattern on the wall that pointed to a duplex outlet. The set was great.

Ron asks me if I could see anything out of place, or if they needed to add anything. He also told me that he and everyone on the movie had a great regard for my opinion and that Robert DeNiro couldn't say enough how much I had helped him in his role as Fire Investigator Rimgale.

Ron said, "If you see anything that does not look good, please tell me."

We looked around. I told them that this explosion blew out the windows and instead of oblong pieces of glass that they need to have thin, long pieces called shards of glass. There were now about ten people listening and taking notes. The pictures in the hallway were still hanging straight and so on.

I had told my brother, Mike, to meet me at the Uptown. He was outside standing by the car when Bob and I came out, and I introduced him and his friend. My brother, Mike, is also with the fire department. He is the director of media affairs.

We drove down Broadway, making small talk, and Bob mentioned that there was an outdoor cafe that he wanted to go to. I drove around but we never found it, and since it was getting late, about 3:30 P.M., we went back to the Ritz. Bob said set call was at 8:00 P.M. and told me to get some rest.

July 29, 2000 Hours

When I arrived back at the set, everyone was in a good mood. A few people came up to me and said, "You and Bob DeNiro were at the Uptown Theater today."

It felt good to be recognized.

Bob was already there by the time I walked over to the trailer. I went in.

Ilona was working on something and Bob was sitting on the sofa. He said tonight was going to be a little deal with him and Stephen, Kurt Russell. He called it an over the shoulder shot.

I asked him if he needed me, told him that Suzi was there and I was going to get a coke or something.

Bob said not to worry, if he needed me he would get me.

I was wearing wing tip shoes and Bob still wanted to be dressed like me, but everyone insisted he should wear navy type shoes.

Bob and I went back to the set in front of the brownstone, met with Ron, and discussed the next shot. The scene was about Kurt going back after the fire, to see what DeNiro was looking for.

We did this scene (take) over and over, the deal being Stephen felt that "Shadow" knew something about the fire, but wasn't going to give a definitive determination as to the cause of the fire at that time. So it was still under investigation because Ron did not want to give the cause away so soon.

Bob called me back to the trailer and he said he was done with this scene, and that he was thankful for all the work and help that I had given him all week. Bob offered me a beer and he also had one, and we sat on the sofa and talked about what we had done so far and what we had to do next week at the Uptown. Bob was happy that we would be going on days. One more beer and he thanked me once again. His car pulled up to take him back to the Ritz Carlton.

After he had left, I walked around looking for Suzi. I met the producer of the movie, Mr. Lewis, near the Craft Service, which is in essence a commissary where you can get a can of pop, coffee, a sandwich or any type of fruit.

Richard Lewis, the producer, stated to me that he had never seen anyone that Robert DeNiro had taken to as easily as he had with me. This made me feel so good, to think that I was well liked and that my opinions were respected.

Suzi was around somewhere, and I went looking for her when they told me that she was going to be an extra in the last scene. I was really tired by this point, so we left the set at 4:00 A.M. and got to bed at 5:00 A.M...What a day!

Saturday, July 21

At ten in the morning Bob called and asked me if I knew any firemen that had been burned.

"Yes, Bob Hoff."

He said he would like to meet him and maybe see his burn scars, because in his part in the movie, as Rimgale, he was burned in a fire and this was why he was transferred to the Fire Investigation Unit. I called Bob Hoff where he was working at the fire house. Bob Hoff was the chief of the 6th battalion, and he agreed to meet with Bob DeNiro in Humboldt Park.

I picked DeNiro up at the Ritz Carlton and we met with Chief Hoff at the east entrance to the park. We sat in Hoff's car and after introducing him to DeNiro they talked about how Hoff got burned in the fire. Also, he showed him the burns on his back. The whole time we talked, DeNiro had his tape recorder going. DeNiro also wanted to know how Hoff felt about being back to working at fires again.

Hoff said that at first it had been hard, but that he had put it—the injuries—behind him and that now he felt comfortable about it.

Bob Hoff is one of those people that are just always going to be a firefighter. No matter what!

At Bob Hoff's home, on another day, I took photos of the burns on his back so that Robert DeNiro would get some ideas for his make-up people.

As we drove down Lake Shore Drive, Bob said how much he liked Chicago. We talked a little about one movie that he had just finished, *Guilty By Suspicion*. We were sitting outside the Ritz, and Bob told me how he had decided that *Backdraft* was a movie for him.

He said, "If a story is good and there is something basically true or interesting, and the character needs to be developed, depending on the director, then I want to be a part of this because it is going to be something special."

That made me feel kind of special.

Sunday

Bob called to see how I was doing and said that if I needed anything, to please call. He explained that he wasn't sure about set call time but that we had to be at the Uptown at about 9:00 A.M. If there were any fires that we should respond to, I shouldn't hesitate to call, otherwise we would meet at 0900 at the theater.

Sunday afternoon I met with Deputy Fire Commissioner Alletto, who had been guiding my step as technical consultant. I filled him in on what we—Bob and I—had been doing up until then with *Backdraft* and the theory of the magnesium and trychtichlorate in the outlet. He was impressed. To impress him, Chief Alletto, with his vast experience, it had to be good. Greg Widen, the screenplay writer of the story, I salute. He was excellent. I told Chief Alletto about the next *Backdraft* scene at the Uptown, and he gave me some more tips from his tremendous bag of knowledge and experience.

Monday, July 23 Uptown Theater

The mood was so much better because the cast and crew all liked to work days. As soon as I got there, people began asking me about Bob and were we still going to fires at night.

I told them, "Yes, Mr. DeNiro never stops working. He is a tireless worker when it comes to acting out a part, a perfectionist, if you will."

I walked around to the trailer, to talk to Bob, but when I got there the guard told me that there was a hold on Mr. DeNiro until that afternoon.

I went over to the Craft Service, and Ron Howard called for me to meet with him in the theater. I went right in to find Mr. Howard.

He asked me if I could help out with a rescue that had to be performed on the fire escape in the rear of the building.

Since Bob wouldn't be on the set till 12:00, I said, "Sure, no problem."

I had my fire gear in the car and I met Ron in the rear by the fire escape. He asked me how I would go about effecting the rescue of a woman from the third floor who was out on the fire escape, and stepped out so the stairs would come down right in front of the camera.

We made the rescue about eight times in full gear, and it was hot. I was really sweating!

Ron thanked me and said, "I hope Bob won't mind."

I replied, "I'm sure he won't."

Ron also asked me to show Scott Glenn how to perform mouth-to-mouth on a lady, which I did.

Bob pulled in at about 12:00 and we went into the trailer. I told him about working with Ron.

He asked me if I liked it, and I told him it was good and that it made me feel good to help out with parts that other people could not do, like walking out on the fire escape stairs and bringing down the woman, since these were normal occurrences in firefighting.

Exterior Theater Scene #93

We brought the fire sedan to the front of the boarded up theater and Bob asked me which tools we should take into the building, as we were looking at the tools in the tool box. Billy Baldwin came alongside of Bob and asked how it was going and what were we doing. Then Ron Howard came up to explain what he wanted the two actors to do.

Ron explained that Brian (Billy's character) was new and was dumped on Rimgale by city hall, that the fact that it was a "political appointment" did not go over well with Rimgale. There were not the best feelings between them. So Rimgale loads Brian down with tools and boxes of investigative equipment.

They went through this part about five times, each time with the fire gear on; then the next time with just fire boots and helmets. Bob asked me, if the fire was out, would I still wear my fire gear?

"I would for safety reasons," I replied.

Well, to make a long story short, Mr. DeNiro wore a fire coat and Brian (Billy) didn't wear any gear. So, it just goes to show you no matter what was right or what was wrong, they still do it the way the director says to do it!

Interior Theater Scene #94

Bob entered at the rear of the theater with Billy and Greg Widen, the writer of the movie. Bob asked me what to do.

I said, "You get as much information about the fire from the officer of the first due engine company and the first due battalion chief."

In this case, Greg Widen is the lieutenant and he tells you the name of the fire fatality, "Cosgrove!"

Interior Theater

Now we get to the victim (Cosgrove). The body is under a door and some theater seats are all burned badly. Bob said, "How are we going to reveal the victim to make it look real?"

(Note: take your time).

He asked, "So I uncover him slow, fast or what?"

I told him, "It does not matter as long as you make it look like you have done it before and it does not bother you. You examine the body close because you're looking for some type of clue."

We repeated this scene about ten or fifteen times before Ron called it a wrap, and we returned to the trailer and had some refreshments.

Bob told me that he wanted to go through the dailies, which were the shots we had done the other day at the brownstone. I said I would love to, and Ilona asked someone where they were, and she wrote the address for me.

Erie and State Streets

I pulled the fire sedan across the street from this plush all glass building. I waited for Mr. DeNiro's white caddie and as soon as he got out so did I, because I didn't know where I was going but I knew Bob did. As we entered the building, there was a doorman and he told us what elevator to take. The lobby was all black marble with shrubs in planters, and we proceeded to the elevators...it was ultra luxurious.

Once on the fourth floor, we were met by the producer, Richard Lewis, and co-producer, Larry DeWaay, who escorted Mr. DeNiro into a small theater. We had some refreshments and snacks, and made small talk until Ron Howard arrived on the scene with his wife and children.

We were given seats. I sat right in front of Mr. DeNiro with Ilona alongside of me. I could not believe I was there.

Mr. Howard gave a hand sign and the lights went dim. I was now watching part of the movie *Backdraft*. Each scene was done over and over, and when the part about "mice with matches" came on, everyone laughed and said it was a good line. When Robert DeNiro leaned up in his seat and tapped me on the shoulder, I turned to look at the grin on his face. It was worth a million bucks. (Here's to you, Norm Doolan.)

41

When it was over, we stood around for a few minutes. Bob said he was going but asked me if I wanted to stay with Ron.

I said, "Nope. You go, I go."

Bob said that he wanted to walk back to the Ritz, which was a few blocks east of where we were. Ilona called me later to ask about my awards. She said that Bob would like to see them. He was very impressed by the awards I had received for saving people from burning buildings.

Mr. DeNiro called that night to ask me if I had my call sheet for Tuesday, 7/24/90. He said we could go over the bulb that they fixed up on the light in the hall entrance, where Rimgale is referring to on the recorder.

Tuesday, July 24

Make-up and hair was at 0800. The sun was out and people were in better moods.

I met Bob and Ilona in front of Rimgale's trailer. We talked over the next scene, about the light bulb that distends toward the heat source, because we had to turn down a hallway to find the point of origin of the fire. Ron had asked me if there are any indicators that show you or point to something and I told them that a light bulb in a fire will begin to melt when 900° is applied for ten minutes and distend or point towards the heat source.

We had some fresh fruit and then Bob had to start make-up. Every day Ilona had to make sure that his make-up and hair, clothes, shoes, watch, everything was perfect or Mr. DeNiro does not leave for the set until every part of his "character" is ready to go on that screen.

There was not a lot of room on the set for everyone that needed to be there, so I waited with Ilona and was given a headset by Mr. Williams, the sound mixer, so I could hear what Mr. DeNiro was saying. When he was relating to the recorder and then to the light bulbs, Bob was great. He put this little extra in when he said, "You sneaky son-of-a bitch," with a whisper in his voice and looking straight at the light bulb.

Lunch Time

Bob didn't eat with us because he was on a special diet. He was getting ready for his next movie, *Cape Fear*. The movie *Backdraft* had 160 people working that day, and when they sat you down for lunch, you were well satisfied by the excellent food and the service; it was just great!

The next scene was a very difficult one because water was dripping and it was about 95 degrees outside. I was called from the set, because they needed the fire car for the sunset shot. I pulled the car around to the side of the theater and was told that the windshield was tinted. When I returned to the set, Mr. DeNiro told me that they couldn't shoot the scene through tinted glass. Bob told me that they would fix it for the next scene.

I was always giving Bob this reason for lines of dermarcation where the smoke on walls were indicators of where the point of origin may well have been. Now I know the reason, because the entrance area scene was perfect. The smoke stains on the walls looked just like the fire scenes that I have been to so many times.

The theater was dirty and had been abandoned for many years. By then it was late afternoon. After many takes in the little hall, we all moved into the small room and the area of the fire's origin, to discuss that the *Backdraft* took place in there and as a result of the explosion, there were shards of glass, and last but not least, there was the duplex outlet same as in the first fire. This part went well since the inside of this particular room was smaller than the entrance. There were only two actors, Bob DeNiro and Billy Baldwin, in this scene and the camera crew.

During the scenes in the hallway of the theater, and in the small room at the end of the shooting, the temperature was 95 degrees outside, and I would say that the temperature in that hallway was +100 degrees. I had felt bad about telling Bob that I always wear my fire coat when I am in the structure. Robert DeNiro wore the heavy fire coat all day.

The director, Ron Howard, monitored the actors in the hallway outside the little office room. Mr. Howard called out that, "It's a take," which finished the inside the theater shooting.

We went back to Bob's trailer.

Once inside the trailer, Bob started to explain some things about how this movie was being worked for him (Mr. DeNiro) so that he could finish on time to begin his next movie, *Cape Fear*. He also told me that it had been very hard in that hallway for everyone.

The crew had to be on location for many hours before each scene was ready for the director and the actors. Each time we moved down the hallway, it would take 45 minutes to set up the next scene. The temperature was in the 90's that day, and that was real hard for everyone.

He said that he wanted to lay down for a while, until the next scene, where we would be riding into the sunset inside the fire sedan.

I left the trailer and went to see how the car was on the side of the theater. When I saw the car, it was overloaded with lights and cameras riding on the outside of each side door. The front of the car was connected to a movie type tow truck by a tow bar and there were cameras mounted on both sides. I went over to the canteen to have something to drink and found out that the next scene had to be perfect into the sun.

They alerted us that we had about ten minutes. I went back to the trailer.

Ilona was sitting outside the trailer. She said, "They have to do make-up for this scene, but come in. Bob wants to talk to you."

Bob said that any fires that we would go to now would have to be during the day because he had been getting up at 4:00 A.M. to start a training program for his next movie, *Cape Fear*. He had to have a lot of muscles in his arms and back.

I told him that I understood.

While we were talking, I looked over and there was his script. In both margin areas of the page was all the writing in Mr. DeNiro's work. He really worked hard, studying lines and parts for the upcoming scene.

Ilona was fixing his hair and make-up, when the knock came at the door.

I answered it; it was the assistant director. "We're ready for Mr. DeNiro now," he said.

As we were walking together, Bob told me that he would need me at this set and asked me to ride on the tow truck with a headset on. I climbed on the truck, then Mr. DeNiro and Billy Baldwin took their positions in the car. I didn't have a clear view of Bob at this time.

Glenn Williams fitted me with a headset so that I could hear what they were saying in the car. Bob was looking around and saying that he could not see "Cos," so I was moved over and up a little so that Bob and I were in eye contact.

We started out at Diversey and Clark where there is a turn around. Heading west into the hot afternoon sun, Ron Howard said "ACTION" and Bob began relating to Billy the properties of magnesium and trychichlorate, driving the car and handing Billy the investigation manual. We went west to Ashland, turned around and did the same take over again four times.

In between takes, we would stop to fix a camera or a light. Bob often would look up and ask me how it had sounded to me on my headset. Then he was telling Billy something. When he realized that the sound was still on, he signaled me and told me to always let him know when the sound was on or off. I later found out that he was giving Billy some tips on something and he did not want anyone listening.

We went back to the trailer.

At the end of another hard day, Bob asked me if I wanted a drink. "You bet," I said.

In the trailer, Ilona was cutting up some limes, placing them around a small plate. In the center she poured salt. Then she took three shot glasses from the freezer and filled them with tequila and handed me a cold bottle of Corona Extra beer.

Bob told me how you first take a wedge of lime, place it in the salt, then bite it. Then you take the tequila and drink it. Then you put the rind of the lime into the bottle of Corona Extra beer.

This system worked well for a while.

We talked about finding this person that was burned because the make-up would have to start testing things for the burns that Bob would have on his arms and back. Ilona gave me the Polaroid camera to take the photos of Bob Hoff's burns.

Another round of limes and beer. I forgot the system; if I was to bite the lime, stick it in the salt, drink or what. I just had the beer.

Bob was laughing by then.

I just said, "I'm Irish. We don't drink this way."

We sat around and talked about our families, our kids. My children could not wait to meet him.

Bob told me that his son might come to the set the following week. His son, Raphael was 13 years old.

It was getting late. Ilona called Todd and again Robert DeNiro thanked me for everything, got into the white caddie and said that set call was at 0730 at the firehouse.

I took the sedan to fill it with fuel. As I was sitting there, I started to realize that I was now an important part of the movie and also a good friend to Mr. Robert DeNiro.

Later on, I received a page from Ilona Herman and, after calling her back, she asked me if I had a fire axe or if I could get one for Robin Chambers in New York.

I told her that I would bring it tomorrow to the set.

That night, I called Bob Hoff and asked him if I could take some photos of the burns on his back, arms, and legs. Bob Hoff and I sat around and talked about the DeNiro experience.

Friday, August 3

Firehouse at 43rd and Paulina; Engine 49's old house. It was a sunny day and a new location. The theater had been a very hard place to work. It had been vacant for some eight years and was a dirty place to work. I was happy to be out of there.

The trailer was parked in the lot on the east side of the firehouse. It was about 20 minutes ride for me and that was alright, when compared to the one hour ride every day to the theater.

Bob arrived about 7:30. We had coffee in his trailer. I went into the firehouse to look around. It was amazing what they had done to the inside. In the front they had Engine 51 stored for a second engine shot on the high-rise fire. The back of the house was three offices with Bob's office right off the back door of the firehouse. His office had awards and certificates that I had given to him to show his character as a fireman that has been around for a long time. We didn't have a set call for about two hours, so I visited with friends Matt Moran, my captain in the Office of Fire Investigation. I introduced them, he and his wife Jan, to Robert DeNiro.

At 9:00 A.M. Mr. DeNiro was called on to the set. Since I knew where the set was, we looked at one another. I said I would lead. Bob had to stop many times on the way into the set to say Hi to chiefs and their wives and kids.

Once inside, Bob asked about the telegraph system, how it worked.

Robert DeNiro and the author. The insription says "Bill ("Cos")
thanks for everything, my friend! Bob"

I briefly explained the system and how we received our calls
in the system, and how well it worked.

Once we were back in the office where the first scene was to
be taken, Bob looked around at some of the tokens in the office.
When he came to the awards, he looked over and said, "These are

your awards," with a DeNiro grin that let me know he approved.

He asked me what the desk should look like, neat and clean or messy.

I said, "You're not a paper fireman, so it is not a mess but busy."

He moved some of the books on to the desk, shuffled some paper and said, "Hey Cos, how does this look?"

I gave him a nod and we both started to laugh.

Ron Howard came into the office to tell Bob some last minute things about the shot. The probie, Peter Herbert, was in the door. Bob was behind the desk and Ron said, "ACTION."

Bob was supposed to yell at this probie for breaking a window before the engine had water. It was the first time I saw Mr. Robert DeNiro the actor.

The scene went as follows: Rimgale was yelling at the probie fireman when Brian, Billy Baldwin, walks in to meet Rimgale for the first time. The first few times Bob yelled, after asking me, "How hard do I yell?"

I'd said, "You have to chew his ass out. This guy almost got everyone killed."

Ron asked everyone to take their places.

I walked around to the back of the camera, and as I was watching Bob, he had turned to face toward the camera. He had made his face all red and puffy and then they called "ACTION".

Robert DeNiro chewed this guy a brand new ass! The cast and crew gave him a big ovation. As we walked back to the trailer, people were shaking his hand and taking photos, Bob was talking to firemen and their families, and he felt good about portraying a fireman.

Once we got back to the trailer, I had to tell him that I had never seen it so real and so I called that scene "The Probie Scene".

We talked about the scene that was next up. Bob asked if taking the shirt off in the office and changing into the uniform had been done in our office. It was funny because Bill Alletto was always doing this same thing every day. Bob never missed when it came time to ask a question about saying, "I knew your father. He had a hell of a reputation on this job." Bob would want to know about the reputation part and I explained that a fireman who has a good reputation in the City of Chicago, can go and work anywhere on his reputation as a fireman. He was always interested in what I had to say about a subject and thanked me for telling him. He said, "Cos, I bet you have a good reputation," with a smile.

Lunch Time

Bob was on a special diet for his next movie, *Cape Fear*, but told me to meet him after lunch in the make-up trailer.

The crew ate about a two block walk down Paulina Street. When I was asked to sit with Ron Howard for lunch, I was thrilled. It was a large table with about 20 people and Mr. Howard said, "Sit here, across from me," Ron ate with the crew, that means 140 people for lunch. All the time he asked me how I was doing with Bob.

I told him it was just fine.

Ron said that he never heard of Robert DeNiro being so close with one of his technical advisors the way he was with me. "The scene he did that morning with the Probie," Ron said, "was great and shows what a terrific actor he is."

The next thing I knew, it was time to get back to meet Mr. DeNiro at the make-up trailer. Once I entered the trailer, Bob called me over to ask how the burns looked. Ilona and a make-up artist, Bob Norin, were applying the burns on Bob's back. He asked me what I thought and I said, "That is great. They look real."

After about two hours of being bent over with both of his arms up in the air, making small talk to me about people who have been burned, he would work on his lines to himself. He always had the script in front of him. Many times I would leave because they were all working. Bob had to wear a loose shirt into this scene, because it was hot outside and with the lights on the set, it was over 100 degrees. At the firehouse I opened the back door that led into the office, to make it easier to get to the set.

Ilona said, "When we go in there, we're not stopping, go straight to the set."

They told me that they needed Mr. DeNiro in ten minutes. When I got back to the make-up trailer, they had finished applying the burns on Bob.

He asked, "How does it look? Is it realistic, like Bob Hoff's?"

I replied, "You look like you need an ambulance."

We all laughed and Ilona said, "Let's go."

I told Bob we had to go around the back.

He said, "Cos, lead the way."

Once inside the firehouse, Ron was ready to call the scene when the burn make-up started to peel off a little, and Bob started getting "pissed." Ilona worked it out, and they shot the scene about six times.

Back in the trailer, I said, "All that work for just that shot."

Bob said that a scene like that would be on the screen for about ten seconds, and maybe would get cut out altogether.

We sat around in Bob's trailer and made small talk. Ilona called for the car.

Bob said he was tired from getting up so early. He was into a full workout training at 4:00 A.M. and then to the set. When we left, I too was very tired.

August 4, My Birthday

It was Saturday, the 12th day of shooting the movie. I arrived at 7:30 A.M. at the firehouse, at 43rd and Paulina. The crew was already busy getting the set ready for the first scene take.

Robert DeNiro on the staircase in the firehouse (where the
author works) at 1401 S. Michigan Ave.

Bob arrived at about 8:00 A.M. and was in a good mood. He
said that he'd had a good workout that morning, with his train-
er Dan. We talked about getting some much needed rest because
of the many nights we had been up until 3 and 4 A.M.

Inside Mr. DeNiro's trailer, we had coffee and talked about
the next scene. Bob said, "It's a small but very important part."

Then came the questions.

Bob asked, "Does this stuff go on in OFI? When a guy leaks a
story to the newspaper, can he get into trouble?"

I related to him that this happens, "Not often, but when it
does happen the shit hits the fan."

Then Bob asked if a guy could get fired for letting this type of
story out.

52

I told him, "No one would get fired, but his ass would be transferred that day since OFI is a resume position."

Still asking questions, he started getting ready for the scene. Ilona would start thumbing through this ring of photos.

Ilona takes a Polaroid photo before each scene and would then match the shirt, pants, shoes, hair and make-up to the prior scene. During this time, I would step out of the trailer because Mr. Robert DeNiro would now be preparing himself for the scene. Although he would always say to me, "You don't have to go, Cos," I knew by then that when he was getting ready to do the next scene that he was doing a lot of thinking, and I didn't want to disturb his thought process.

We made our way into the firehouse to meet Ron Howard, the director, and Billy Baldwin. They talked to each other about the shot, then Ron gave them some last minute details about the take.

Bob started with throwing the morning paper on the desk. With a soft but firm voice, and an irritated expression and some sarcasm, Mr. "D" was in his world. I don't know what else to say, he simply loves making movies, and really gets into his part.

Back in the trailer, Bob said he had some calls to make. I wanted to give him some privacy, so I went to get coffee at the Craft Service, where Ron Howard was also having coffee. He told me that Bob was "great!" Ron Howard told me again that we were really doing a great job together, and that he thought that Robert DeNiro was probably one of the finest actors of his time and that not only he but many of his fellow actors fully agree.

Happy Birthday Billy

When I returned to Bob's trailer, he asked me to come in. I didn't think much about it, but once inside, Bob said, "Happy birthday" with, as always, an embrace and sincerity and genuineness.

53

I was overwhelmed.

Bob handed me a birthday card that he had wrote, a short message with the date and signature. He handed me a bag with ribbon and bows on it and said, "Happy birthday."

Inside the bag was a signed script of the movie and a bottle of Dom Perignon, a cigar made in the Dominican Republic, and a pair of socks to make up for the pair I had given him when he had worn none.

I looked at him and said, "Hey, how about what was said about no gifts on the birthday?"

He said, "I didn't buy any one of these," and we laughed. He said, "After we shoot this afternoon, we'll have a drink."

The next scene started with Bob and Billy Baldwin. DeNiro had started to get his props together, when he realized that the briefcase that had been given to him was not like the one I use. Bob called the propmaster, Dennis Parrish, and told him that he wanted a case like the one Cos carries with him.

Dennis asked to see my case and said that he didn't have anything like that.

"Well, that's what I want," DeNiro said. Then Ron Howard walked over to see what was up, and DeNiro says to the propmaster, "Ask Cos if he will sell you his case."

Dennis asked me, "How much do you want for it?"

I didn't know what to say.

Bob said, "About $125.00," and they said OK. It was a done deal.

Bob and I, we laughed as we walked away. It was great.

The next scene was where Billy commits himself when Bob enters the fire station. After five or six takes Mr. Howard yells, "That's a take. Print it."

The next scene was a *Backdraft* lesson in which Bob is calling to Billy to come over to his side of the firehouse. When he tells him to take the top off of a small metal can, fire instantly blows out about three feet high in the air. Billy jumps back and DeNiro smiles. It was a one scene shot and they pulled it off perfectly! The special effects of the rigged trash can was just great.

We returned to the trailer and Bob asked Billy if he wanted to have a beer on Cos's birthday. Suddenly, I found myself in Robert DeNiro's trailer, being toasted by Bob, Billy Baldwin and Ilona Herman on my birthday. Who could ask for anything more than that?

After Billy left the trailer, we just talked. I told him that my kids were going to be over that day and also that it was the day of our block party!

Bob said he would like to go, and also that he wished that his son Raphael was going to be in that week, but that he wouldn't be in until Monday.

Bob told me that Raphael was 13 years old and was going to spend some time with him. I could tell from the way he spoke about his son that he was real excited, emotional. He said that he would like to take him fishing somewhere, maybe for a day where they would not be disturbed, and asked me if I knew any place to fish.

"We'll find one and make a day out of it," I said.

We talked about our mutual friend, Bob Rice, who had been an advisor to him on the movie *Midnight Run*, and who lived by me on the south side of Chicago. Bob told me where he lived in New York, in an eight story building in Manhattan. On the second floor he owns a restaurant, *The Tribeca Grill*, which is famous, and also the *Tribeca Film Center*. He also has a floor where he stores his wardrobe from the many, many movies that he has been in. He lives on the top floor.

I asked him about any vacations or if he ever just took some time off.

He said that he would take time off later, but that for now he hates to waste any time. He is strong and healthy now, he told me, and there's a time when you're "hot" and everything is working for you, and that this is not a time when you take vacation from your work.

We had another birthday drink and I pointed out that it was after 8:00 P.M.

"I am one hour late for the block party," I said.

Bob said he had made some other plans, but that maybe we could go fishing the following week, on Sunday with his son, Raphael. I thanked him for the nice birthday presents, and he thanked me for the socks and all of my help with the character he was playing.

"We have a new location Monday," he said. He gave me the call sheet and we agreed he would see me there.

August 6

It was the 13th day of shooting, at 7:30 A.M. We were at the Helene Curtiss Building at 325 North Wells Street. All of the trailers were parked in the rear of the building, and we had to enter in the rear by the freight elevator, off a loading dock.

Bob arrived at 8:00 A.M. We stood outside on the sidewalk for about ten minutes and Bob just looked around at the buildings. We went into the trailer to have coffee with Ilona and to get instructions about when they would need Mr. DeNiro on the set.

Bob said, "This is a hard day for a director, with the crew all over the place. We can only use the freight elevator for a certain time and this place is fussy about keeping things clean."

We finished our coffee and I told Bob that I would find us the best way up to the penthouse. When I returned to the trailer, Bob was looking at the call sheet and asked me if I could call Bobby Rice or did I have his number.

I do not normally have a good memory for phone numbers but that morning I remembered Bobby Rice's phone number. I

From left to right: Bill Cosgrove, Robert DeNiro, Ron Howard,
the Director, and Dennis Parrish, the Prop Master.

handed the phone to DeNiro and it rang until Bobby Rice picked
up and said, "Hello."

"Happy Birthday," DeNiro said.

Bobby Rice now, I think, recognized the voice and they
laughed. Bob patted me on the back and said to Bobby, "I was
looking at the call sheet and it says they need a detective for the
part in the movie. Do you want to come down to the set?"

Bobby answered, "YES," and we all laughed.

When the phone conversation was over, Bob and I talked
about Bobby Rice and what a terrible misfortune he had in his
life, with the death of his daughter, Shannon.

That was the second time I had seen this compassion for
people expressed by Robert DeNiro. It was terrific to listen to
him talk about the good time he had with Bobby Rice and that
Bobby was a funny guy. He was DeNiro's friend. After a while
Bob said to me, "People you observe all the time; but the ones

you remember, you put in the back of your head and keep."

Bob notified Ron Howard about Bobby Rice and said he would be there within the hour. I mean, they needed cops; why not Bobby Rice? It was a good thing and DeNiro was happy doing that for Bobby on his birthday. The first time I had seen this compassion was at St. Mary's Hospital with the little girl who was burned playing with matches.

They gave the call that they needed Mr. DeNiro for a scene in ten minutes. I told Bob that we would go up in the lobby elevator that I had found earlier.

In the scene he had to wear an arm sling and his hand was bandaged. He was in full blue fireman's uniform. You know, DeNiro really looked sharp with the uniform white shirt on.

Ilona said, "Wait till you see him dressed up."

She was so right. He really looked like a real fire department officer.

Set call for DeNiro was 10:00 A.M., but no Bobby Rice. I said, "What do you think?"

DeNiro said, "He will be here. Let's walk to the elevator."

Once we were up in the penthouse with Ron, there was some time. Then they did a walk through; from the elevator to a large meeting room with a large oval shaped table, where you could sit 40 people.

Bobby Rice showed up and they gave him a run through of his part.

Ron said, "And ACTION."

They quickly walked out of the elevator and down the hall. It took about six takes before it was a print.

We then all went back to Bob's trailer, talked to Bobby Rice for a while, and then I left them alone to talk privately.

That afternoon we went back up to the set. Bob was to have his photo taken, "still shots," and we got some taken with him. It was really nice of him to let us get in the photos. In the next scene, while he was coming into the large room, he said, "Why did you pay Cosgrove, Holcome and Seagrave to create a phoney manpower study?"

We finished the scene after about six takes, and then we all went back to Bob's trailer to have a "cold one" with Bobby Rice on his birthday.

August 7

The 14th day of shooting and this was our second day at the Helene Curtiss Building. It was only 8:00 A.M., and Bob was to be on the set at 9:00 A.M.

I talked with Ilona. As mentioned previously, Ilona Herman is Robert DeNiro's personal make-up artist and key hair stylist, among many other movie specialties. As the person who schedules his day and his diet, Ilona is also his dietitian. She decided what foods were to be included in Mr. DeNiro's diet for the next movie, which is *Cape Fear*. I am not too sure when, but sometime in her life, Ilona had been a Registered Nurse. She knows about injury and pain, and the way to mend almost anything. I know now that Robert DeNiro is not only a good actor, but he is also a very smart businessman, having a person as good as Mrs. Ilona Herman to handle his important personal business.

Bob arrived and told us that he had been talking to Ron and that we would be moving to a new location after the scene in the hall with Billy Baldwin. There were so many people working in the hall area, that they were asking people not in the scene to please leave.

I asked Bob, "Should I go downstairs?"

Bob said, "No, you stay right here!"

When we returned to the trailer, Bob called his son, Raphael, who had arrived in Chicago and was back at the hotel. He told him that we were going to change locations and to meet him at the Chinatown firehouse on Cermak and Wentworth.

New Location, Chinatown Firehouse

This was the first time I had met Bob's son, Raphael. A very good looking, 13-year-old lad, he was full of energy. Raphael asked all about the fire department and asked me how I had become an investigator and a fireman.

I carefully explained to him how this had come about, and then we went to see the firehouse that was around the corner from Bob's trailer.

There were a lot of people around and the traffic was terrible. This particular firehouse had Engine 8, Truck 4 and the 2nd battalion stationed there. There were firemen all over. Many had stayed on from the previous day's shift just to watch the movie *Backdraft* being made right on their doorstep.

They used only the exterior of the Chinatown firehouse. The interior shots were made at the old firehouse at 43rd and Paulina. The first take was a running shot and they had taken the front seat out of a 1990 Chrysler sedan, with all the cameras mounted like the running shot we had done at the Uptown with the firecar.

There were a lot of people around and Bob wasn't in a good mood. Something had gone wrong during the movie, or maybe it was just the move. He asked me not to stop on the way to the set. He did not want to meet anyone.

There were a lot of firemen there that day from OFI. They wanted to talk and meet him, but that day was not a good day. As we walked toward the car, people were calling out his name and waving to him to stop.

We met with Ron Howard at the sedan. They talked over a few things about not letting on to Swayzak, the alderman who was running for Mayor of Chicago, who by then was afraid because three of his friends were dead from the fires.

Bob told me to get on the camera truck with a headset. Running shots! I was on the camera truck and Bob was in the Chrysler sedan with J. T. Walsh.

Bob asked me if I could hear him OK.

I said, "OK," and we pulled away.

The shot was taken about six times while we went around the block. There was a lot of humor in the scene and—this is my own opinion—I think Robert DeNiro is great at a humor type scene.

We went back to the trailer and Bob made some calls.

I went into the firehouse to meet with some of the guys. I told them why we could not stop before.

They asked me if Robert DeNiro would take a picture with all the guys in front of Engine 8.

I said, "I will ask him."

It took about one hour to change the set to the firecar, OFI, 4-6-8 in front of the firehouse.

He said, "Do you know these guys?"

Bob shot the scene, getting out of the car and meeting with J.T. Walsh in his sedan.

After, I asked Bob to take the photo with the guys. He agreed and took several photos, and then spent some time talking to the firemen.

Ron Howard then said, "IT'S A WRAP!" We were done with what had been a long day with the move.

August 8, 1990

Bob called me in the morning and told me that they would call us when they got finished with the factory fire. "So take the day off," he said, "or if you want to go to the set to watch them shoot, go ahead."

I had a lot to do, what with being off work so long. But I did drive to the set to pick up my call sheet for the next day.

Robert DeNiro and the Fireman

Bob called to tell me that we had to be at the set at 10:00 A.M. That day I brought my wife, Suzi, to the set. She found Ron Howard's wife, and spent the next few hours watching *Backdraft* being made.

The building was an abandoned hospital at 5401 South Morgan. DeNiro did not have to go into the structure. What he did while getting his fire clothes on, was to stall Swayzak and Jennifer in their attempt to get some answers regarding the cause of the fire. While they were asking Bob questions he had to get dressed. His fire clothes were in the trunk of the sedan and he had to tell Swayzak to "get out of the way." Because the character is a fireman he has to be polite to him but by his actions and expressions, you know he doesn't like him.

Chicago Evangelical Hospital Exterior Factory Shot.

One of the lines that Bob had to use was, "Awful expensive shoes to be wearing on the fire ground."

I said to Bob, "It's not 'fire ground'. You should say 'fire scene'.

Bob told Ron, and then thanked me for making the correction.

They finished the scene in about two hours.

Bob was then anxious to meet with his son, Raphael. He said, "Maybe we can do the fishing thing now because we're going to be off Saturday and Sunday." He added, "I will call you tomorrow morning," and he then left the set. I stayed with Suzi for a little while and then we left.

Saturday, August 11

Bob called about 10:00 A.M. and said that day wasn't good

because Raphael had made some plans, but he said that the next day would be better. Then he asked me if I would mind meeting him and Ron and Allen Hall, the special effects coordinator, to work on the scene where we would be using a flammable liquid up the wall on Sunday.

I said OK. I wasn't too sure about the scene, but I told him that I would meet him at the studio.

Sunday, August 12, 1990
Chicago Studio City, Stage #1

It was pouring rain! Ron was thankful that I had come out and said he was so sorry that this would break up our Sunday.

They had built some walls in the studio, an inside corner constructed of drywall. They experimented with a flammable/combustible liquid.

They would make a trail up the wall and across the floor and try to ignite it with a cigarette. It would not ignite with just the hot coal of the cigarette. They needed an open flame, like a match or an electrical spark. Over and over they lit it up with an open flame and then Bob with a portable fire extinguisher would put it out.

We really had a good time. There were many times when the flames would be five feet over the top of the walls. There were only six people working with us.

Ron said, "It's cheaper to do this today than to learn it while paying 150 people." And if we were going to learn what type of flammable liquid, it was safer because we had plenty of fire extinguishers.

I have to say, Bob was getting real good at putting the fires out.

It was about 3:00 P.M. we had coffee, and talked about an ignition source to ignite the flammable liquid.

We finished up at the studio. The rain continued to fall and the weatherman said it would rain all day. So much for our backyard barbecue at my house and fishing. Bob said he had not told Raphael one way or the other, because he didn't know what time we would finish with Ron.

We took the rest of the day off. OH WELL!

Monday, August 13

Fire Station, 1401 South Michigan Avenue, (which was OFI, my firehouse).

Bob was in a very good mood and was meeting all the fire marshals that were changing shifts. We went back to the trailer and talked about the script, the part where he was trying to talk to Stephen about the Report.

I explained to Bob that the most important thing is the Report. "Chief Alletto gives us time, but he wants the report done properly and if it isn't, he can get real tough about that."

The set was on the second floor of the firehouse, in the officer's room. Bob was talking to Kurt Russell about the Reports. First they did a walk through with Ron Howard. Then they took their places, and there was a hush throughout the whole area and Ron says, "ACTION."

The scene took about one or two hours.

We went back to the trailer and Bob said that Ron was trying to shoot the hall of records scene at the Daley Center, and that we might make the move after lunch. Bob told me that if Ron could get the new location, that he could save a lot of time and maybe take two weekends off, because all the night work had taken its toll on the crew. Again, here was Robert DeNiro's personal concern for Ron and the crew. He had been in the business a long time and knew that a move like this could save a lot of money.

We moved to the heart of the Chicago loop. There were people everywhere. Policemen were guiding us into the streets around the Daley Center.

Bob's trailer was parked at the corner of Randolph and Dearborn. Because of the congestion around the Daley Center, they had to put the trailers on all four sides of the Center. There was a traffic jam and a big crowd problem.

The set was on the 10th floor, which houses part of the huge Cook County Circuit Court system of Illinois, and is also the floor where Aurelia Pucinski's office is located. Ms. Pucinski is the elected Clerk of the Circuit Court.

By the time I reached the trailer, Bob was already preparing for the next scene. I knew that they were going for a time frame of sunset, similar to the scene in the fire car, when they had been in the car driving into the sunset toward the hall of records. We had an older policeman as the escort into the building.

It was hot and Bob seemed like he didn't like the idea of all the people around. Once inside the building, there were twice as many people as outside. When we were in the elevator, there must have been ten people in the elevator with Bob. Ilona said to me, "I wish we could do something about this. It is a bad distraction for Bob."

When we reached the 10th floor it was better. The crew and about 150 extras were in this big office of Aurelia Pucinski's. Bob said to me that Billy Baldwin got caught by 100 people downstairs.

Ron Howard explained that in this particular scene they were looking for "records" of the company that was running the scam.

In the meantime, I started to look around for a better way out.

There was a man looking through the window of an office door. As I approached him, he started to leave. I asked this man if there was a better way out or another elevator, even the freight elevator.

The man explained to me that he wasn't supposed to be up on this floor but knew a good way down. He asked me if he could watch to see if any actors would come over there.

I told him that if he could get me down the back elevators, that he not only would see an actor, but he would meet Robert DeNiro.

I went back to the set, where I met with Ilona. I told her that I had found a better way down.

Bob came over and said that they would have to shoot three different directions, which meant three set-ups with about a half hour between each scene.

I told him that I got the elevator.

Bob said, "One more shot of this scene, and we will go back to the trailer."

When the scene was over, Bob looked at me and I gave him a small nod, indicating that we would go out this way. There was no hesitation. Bob started toward me and Ilona was right behind him.

Once we left the large office, we went down a huge corridor that had a bank of elevators at the end of it. At the last elevator, there was the man waiting for us.

We entered his elevator and I introduced Bob to him. This fellow worked for the County as a maintenance man. Bob was very nice to this guy as he is to most people. He thanked him for bringing us down and asked him how long he had worked in the building and about his family. This made the man feel really good.

Once on the ground floor, the fellow also showed me how to walk out onto the Dearborn side of the building. It was so easy; we never saw anyone.

The next scene was about an hour later. Bob went into his trailer, and I went over to the Craft Service to get some coffee. The officer that was assigned to Mr. DeNiro asked me, "Where the hell is he at?"

The author on the back of the camera truck during the shooting of the film.

"He is in the trailer," I responded.

Bob thanked me for finding a new way in and out of the building.

"The large crowd is such a distraction to him," Ilona said, "because of his lines and his actions during a shooting."

After a while, we went back up to the 10th floor of the Daley

Center two more times, with the special help of that great guy in the elevator.

It had been a long day and we talked about the new scene location for the following one.

Bob asked me if I had a call sheet.

Well, by that time in the movie, I knew enough to have one.

Bob thanked me again for getting him in and out of the Daley Center.

"I was glad to have been of service," I said.

The white caddie pulled up. It was Todd. He asked me if there was a birthday party for Mr. DeNiro.

I said that Ilona had mentioned something, but it wasn't for sure, and that Robin was going to be in, and we would know tomorrow.

Tuesday, August 14

It was the 20th day of shooting. The new location was St. Anne's Hospital, 4900 West Thomas...a hospital that was closed several years ago, over on Chicago's west side.

Bob asked me how or what makes a hospital close. He said, "You know that they are needed."

I replied that in all probability, it was rising supply and labor costs, and perhaps poor management, among other things.

It was a large complex of buildings spread out over an entire city square block. I told Bob about the fire that had taken the lives of 93 children at Our Lady of the Angels school. Most of the victims had been brought to that hospital.

Bob's trailer was parked on the lawn in a very quiet place. This looked like it was going to be a good location for Ron. He wouldn't have to move for a while. Moving around cost big bucks. That's what Bob says. I had mentioned something to Bob about a saying that would go in the next scene and we worked on it while we were walking to the set, which was down a long hallway and up a dirty stairway. Some of the places that the movie worked at: if I ever hear anyone say that the movies are all glamorous and pretty, I will have to tell them.

On the outside stairs, Bob tried out the line in which Ronald says he likes telephones (because he didn't have any toys when he was a kid). Bob liked the saying and tried to get in each time. However, when they did the scene, it came out wrong and they left it out.

Oh Well!

All of the work on the Chicago so-called arsonist, "Fat Albert," had been for this scene. Although they were never introduced, the great actor, Donald Sutherland, portrayed him perfectly, as a strange misfit that knew Rimgale and the way that the fire department operated. The scene also defined how Rimgale got the name "Shadow", when he saved the life of arsonist Ronald Bowland—Sutherland—and the scene also explained how Rimgale was burned, and the scars on his arms and back are brought out.

Ron Howard introduced me to his brother, Clint, who played the part of a medical examiner in the city morgue. He asked Bob if he could pick my brain about burn victims that are in the morgue.

DeNiro told Clint Howard, "If anyone knows about burn victims it is Cos and he has an on-going relationship with the Medical Examiner."

I went with Clint to the Craft Service area and had coffee. He asked me about "rigor mortis" and how soon it actually begins after a fire, and many other things about fire deaths.

Ron Howard called for the next scene, which was the parole board scene where Rimgale prevents Ronald from getting his parole after spending time in prison for arson. Bob told me that the scene was supposed to be in the morning, so in order to make it look like morning they would use two condors or lifts with lights that would shine in the windows of the court room and creates a "daylight" look. It did.

We sat around in the trailer after Bob was finished shooting the parole board scene. We talked about how much time was left for Bob on the movie. Bob told me that the next scene was to be in the morgue and that also would be in St. Anne's Hospital.

Ilona asked me if I would give her a ride back to the Ritz Carlton. While I was driving Ilona Herman back to the hotel, she told me that they were going to have a birthday party for Bob and she told me to bring my wife. Ilona also stated that Robin would be there and that she was bringing the fire axe that I had given her when we were at the theater. As we drove through the city, we made small talk about various things.

I asked Ilona, "Does Bob have a birthday party each year?"

She said, "No, he never has a birthday party," and that it would be a very select group of people who would be invited.

As I drove home, I thought to myself, 'Here I am, being asked to a private party for Mr. DeNiro, after only knowing him for some 35 days. Here is a man that is renowned throughout the world as a great actor...an Academy Award winner...and I'm invited.'

Many of his fellow actors have stated that Bob is most probably the finest actor of his time. I did not say anything to anyone other than my wife Suzi that I was going to the party, because Ilona said not to let anyone know about it.

St. Anne's Hospital. To me a movie set looks a lot like a fire scene because of all the equipment that is needed to support the making of a movie. There are also thick electrical lines that supply lights, sound and many other needs at a movie scene. All of the lines lead to the set, not unlike a fire scene, where all the hoses lead to the fire.

That day they would try to finish the scene in the prison interview room. We only worked until 3:00 P.M. When Bob left the set, so did I. To have the rest of the afternoon and evening off was a treat for me.

The next day they did the morgue scene. I was called on the pager to call the movie set office, and they told me that someone from city hall would be coming to the movie set that day. "Will you please introduce her to Robert DeNiro?" they asked.

The set was on the second floor of St. Anne's. They turned a large room, which I think was normally used as a recovery room, into the city morgue. Bob was very impressed with the set.

There were two carts upon which the bodies of Cosgrove & Seagrave lay. They were covered with plastic. Bob and I went over to the side and he asked me what I do when I follow-up in the morgue.

I told him that, "We are only there to view the bodies and to learn any pertinent information about the condition of the victim's body."

The charred corpses were real looking. Bob asked if I would touch the bodies.

"NO! Any time you have to touch anything you wear plastic gloves."

We talked about getting the gloves on Billy Baldwin because he would have to touch the bodies, to make it look realistic.

The person from city hall showed up. I went to meet her on the first floor. I asked Bob, "Could she watch for one scene?"

Of course. He looks at her and says, "YES!"

She was a very good looking woman, about 30 years old. I introduced her to Bob. They talked a little, then Ron Howard said, "ACTION!"

We all talked about her for a time. She was a bright spot, since there had been a lot of gloom in the morgue until she arrived. I forgot her name. I should have kept it in with my notes.

The rest of the day went by and we had to move to the first floor. Bob was in a hospital bed, and I wasn't sure if he was mad at something or at someone, but he was pissed, and as the scene developed so did DeNiro. He was flaming red-faced and mad as hell because he couldn't find out: Who was this person that was causing the backdrafts? Now Rimgale was almost one of the victims after he had saved Brien and Swayzak.

August 16, St. Anne's

We were sitting in the trailer, talking about the Middle East and I told Bob that my son, Tim, was in the navy and that they had gone on alert.

Bob said that most of the news was about Iraq invading Kuwait on August 2nd, 1990. Bob asked me what ship Tim was serving on and what type of job he had on the ship. He was always concerned about how I felt about the war situation. My son's ship was an amphibious landing ship, called the USS New Orleans.

I said, "You know when they talk in the news about the USA going over there? I just would never be too concerned, but now knowing that it could be my son, Tim, now that scares the shit out of me!"

That was the last day at St. Anne's Hospital. We would be moving to the back lot of Chicago Studio City, Stage #1.

Bob told me about Saturday night, his birthday party, and asked me to be there, said that he was looking forward to my being there. Then he said good-bye.

Bob's Birthday August 17, 1990

Chicago Studio City
5660 N. Taylor
Stage #1
I met Bob when he arrived and wished him a happy birthday.

We had coffee, and since he is a very shy man, he asked me not to spread the word that it was his birthday, I understood and mentioned it to no one.

The scene was back with the OFI toolbox, and the crowbar popping the molding from around a door frame. The set was manufactured to look like the interior of an office high-rise that had had an explosion from a backdraft. As Ron Howard escorted Mr. DeNiro and Billy Baldwin through the offices, I looked around, and I was impressed with the way it looked...just like a *real* fire scene.

Bob looked at me with a smile when I complimented Ron.

Interior of Stage #1 at Studio City.

Bob and Billy Baldwin were conducting their investigation when a woman walked into the mess. They found out that she was the secretary of the third fire victim, Jeff Holcomb! She started rambling about that he was the owner of this building and was the Darth Vader of tax accountants, and a real sleazeball.

In the afternoon, there was a shot with Bob and Kurt Russell! When Kurt was distraught over "Tim", one of the firemen in his Company that was severely burned as a result of the backdraft, his acting was really convincing.

We finished at about 3:00 P.M. and returned to Bob's trailer, where Ilona had prepared a few drinks for the three of us. I wished Bob a "Happy Birthday," shook his hand and left. Ilona reminded me that the next day we would be going to the Chicago Fire Department Shops.

Robert DeNiro and the Fireman

August 18, Fire Department Shops, 31ST & Sacramento

I arrived at the shops rather early, in order to look for some of the firemen that I worked with. At 0800, Mr. DeNiro's trailer was out front, and the set was in the middle of the shops.

The Shop is a large, two story, open repair facility, that had fire trucks on lifts that were being worked on. The movie had called the workers back in on Saturday to shoot the scene. They met with the director, Ron Howard, and he walked through the scene with them.

In it a fire engine pulls out, and Bob and Billy follow, all the time talking about false reports. The scene took most of the morning, and some of the firemen in the shops asked if they could take a photo with DeNiro.

I went to ask Bob, and he said, "sure," but only after the scene. Tony Maritato and Frank Leberis had a camera, and we took a few photos. The Crew was moving back to Chicago City Studio, but Bob told me to go home and get some rest for the party that night.

Bob's Birthday Party
Chez Paul, Erie & Rush

I arrived with my wife, Suzi, at about 8:00 P.M. I was asked my name, my car was taken to valet parking, and we were escorted to the room where the party was to take place.

Mr. DeNiro was not there yet, but I was met by Ilona Herman, and then, at last, I was introduced to Ms. Robin Chambers.

Robin is Mr. DeNiro's Executive Assistant. She manages the home office, and anything that will or could happen in Mr.

Bob's Birthday Party (from top left clockwise): Ron Howard,
the author, Robert DeNiro cutting the birthday cake with the fire axe,
and Robin Chambers and Ilona Herman.

DeNiro's business day. Bob could not say enough about her special talents.

I was also introduced to Mrs. Toukie Smith, with whom he has had a long-standing relationship. She told me that Bob could not say enough about me, and how much I had helped him with the movie.

The next person that Ilona introduced me to was this pretty young woman who was Bob's adopted daughter, Drena. Also, I met again with Raphael, Bob's son. I knew that this party was a very private party with only the main people of the movie *Backdraft* invited: Ron Howard and wife, Kurt Russell, William Baldwin, J. T. Walsh, the producer Richard Lewis, and the writer Greg Widen. There were other people at the party, but I did not know most of them.

The food was anything you wanted: fish, prime rib, etc. When dinner ended, the waiter brought in a chrome-plated fire axe that I had given to Ilona weeks before. She and Robin had had the axe chrome-plated, and had an inscription put on the side about the movie and Bob's Birthday. It was the highlight of

J.T. Walsh, one of the actors, asking to lift our
glasses when he set me up.

Robert DeNiro (far right) with the fire axe that was once mine.

- -

the party, and Bob really loved the axe.

The next thing that happened was that a birthday cake was placed on the table in front of Bob. It was in the shape of a fire engine with red frosting. We all sang Happy Birthday, To MR. ROBERT DENIRO! Then, as only he can do with that special style of his...HE CUT HIS BIRTHDAY CAKE WITH THE FIRE AXE!

It was great, and from across the room Bob caught my eye, giving me that smile of approval, and I knew he liked it. With a nod back to him, I felt honored.

J. T. Walsh asked for everyone's attention, and asked if we could all raise our glasses to toast the person whose party this was for, Mr. Robert DeNiro. With glass in hand, J. T. Walsh said that he would like to give the first toast, but it would only be right for Mr. DeNiro's technical advisor, Bill Cosgrove, to do the honors.

I looked at him, and I know that I must have had a surprised look on my face, since I never in my wildest dreams was prepared to give a toast to anyone. And now to have to toast Mr. DeNiro was rather intimidating, but I accepted the challenge. I think it went something like this: "I have been honored to be invited to this special event for a great actor! I also have been honored to have been selected as his technical advisor. When could an ordinary "mutt" fireman like me be this lucky...So, Bob, may you have good health, a long life, great friends, and may all your plans and dreams come true. HAPPY BIRTHDAY, BOB!"

There were many more toasts to Bob, from Kurt Russell, Ron Howard and Billy Baldwin. We sat and listened to Bob as he thanked everyone for being there. As we enjoyed the evening, Bob came over to me and, with the special concern that I have come to know, said thank you to me, and, as always, he embraced me with a big hug.

We had a great time, and I am sure everyone else did too. As the night went on, I noticed who else was embraced like I was, and there were only a couple of people. The next thing I knew, it was all over. We said our good-byes and Ron Howard said that as the director of the movie, set call was at 8:00 A.M., Monday. The women were given roses to take home with them.

Monday, August 20TH
Chicago Studio City
Stage #1

It was time to do the scene that we had practiced before, with the flammable liquid on the doorway.

I met with Bob at the trailer. We sat for a while and had coffee. Bob talked about how great the birthday party had been, and asked me if I'd had a good time. My reply, of course: "It was a great party. Thanks for asking me to be there."

Ron Howard showed Bob and Billy through the scene. It was a small hallway or entrance to the office where the backdraft had already taken place.

Bob was to take a small plastic container with the flammable liquid, pour it on the floor and on the door, and with a lit cigarette it was supposed to ignite, but it didn't. So special effects set something to ignite the flammable liquid with, and a flash fire came over the top of the door and across the ceiling. Then Bob took a fire extinguisher and put the fire out.

On the way back to the trailer, Bob asked me to stay with him when he was doing this scene, because of the fires.

I told Bob that I thought that this was my job and that, "I will be right there at your side."

The scene took all day to complete. They shot it in two kinds of ways, once from the front of the doors to get the full effect of the flames. It was HOT and the scene was taken about 12 times. Then we broke for lunch while the set was being changed to where the cameras shot through the door jam, and each time it was taken, the fire had to be extinguished, and then set up again. Each time this had to be set up, Bob had to wait. It aggravates him, waiting for things to be changed on the set.

One thing was funny that day. In the scene, Bob had to use a crowbar to loosen the door stop, and while we were waiting to retake the scene, I said to Bob in a joking manner, "Man, are you getting good with that crowbar...it's your best tool."

He said to me, "Back off, Cos, this is not my best tool or my only tool."

We both started laughing again.

It was very hot and some people were getting pissed off about the lack of help after each take. There weren't enough fire extinguishers to put the fires out, and a couple of times the fire scene got a little dangerous. Ron Howard was trying not to burn the set up before he finished his scene and the camera crew had to wear masks because of the amount of smoke that was created from the fires.

After all was done, and the last take was completed at about 7:30 P.M., Ron Howard said, "And that's a wrap!"

Robert DeNiro and the Fireman

Back in the trailer, Bob said to me, "Thank you for everything! It looks like we only have one more scene left to complete. We will move to Swayzak's house in Hinsdale."

Tuesday, August 21
306 East Fist Ave., Hinsdale

I was called to the set a little early because they would be needing the red fire sedan that I had been driving.

I met with Ilona at the trailer. I had asked her if it was alright if I brought my kids to meet Bob, and she said sure, but only for a little while.

Bob met some of my kids and my in-laws. He was just great, asking all of them questions about school, and what they were going to be in the future.

The trailer was far from the set, which seemed to be a problem, because Bob would have to walk about three fourths of a block through a whole lot of people, and that was going to be changed. Bob met Ron on the set for the walk through and, as always, had Billy with him. Nighttime was just setting in, and Ron Howard, as always, had the set just perfect.

The first scene was outside of alderman Swayzak's house, a large, stone, very impressive looking home. The arson car pulled up the driveway, and Bob and Billy got out, walking up to the side door. The shot was done about three times, and then Mr. DeNiro's trailer was moved to the side of this very large house, so he wouldn't have to walk so far.

The next scene was on the interior, where Bob and Billy find the door ajar. There were limitations as to who could be inside as the set was just a small hallway. By then it was past midnight, and most of the spectators went home. The people who owned this fabulous home were the nicest people, Tom and Pat Murphy.

If you needed anything, all you had to do was ask. Ron called it a wrap somewhere about 3:00 A.M.

August 22, Hinsdale 2000 Hours

The next shot or scene was where Billy and Bob smell gas. Billy checked on the gas and got attacked by the BAD guy. They rolled on the floor. There was a duplex outlet that started flashing like the other outlets, and during the fight Billy pushed his attacker against the outlet and burnt him. He hit and knocked Billy out with the club.

Then Bob ran in and fought with the arsonist. DeNiro was thrown against the stair railing and the arsonist ran out the front door. At this point, Bob had to take the unconscious Billy out the front door to the porch.

I was outside with Ilona. Bob called me in and asked me how I would take a guy like Billy Baldwin outside in a hurry and like a firefighter.

The best way that I knew was to lay him on his back and grab him under his arms and pull him out onto the front porch. Once Bob had completed pulling Billy out, he then had to come back into this place where there was going to be an explosion. The gas was flowing free from the space heater and the electrical outlet was sparking and arcing.

Bob crawled into the living room, where Swayzak was in a semiconscious position against the sofa. He helped him to his feet and they started towards the front door.

The last scene was to be shot after the backdraft explosion. There was debris all over the lawn and sidewalk! Robert DeNiro was in a sitting position with the sharp end of a piece of wrought-iron fence through his right shoulder. After the scene was completed, Mr. DeNiro was given a standing ovation from the cast and crew of *Backdraft*.

Bob told me that he would be leaving the set that morning and had to meet his plane at Midway Airport between 05:30 and 06:00.

He told Todd Dickinson that, "Cos knows the best way to the airport. We will follow you, Cos, is that OK?"

I returned to him with lights and siren and he laughed with that special grin of his.

Ilona stayed with the trailer to pack. As I drove through the western suburbs in the red fire sedan, I would look in my rear view mirror to see the white Cadillac following me, only to wonder: When will I ever see Bob DeNiro again?

Butler Aviation
5800 S. Central
Midway Airport

We arrived at the West gate of Midway Airport by the firehouse of Engine 118. After clearing through the security gate, I let the white Cadillac drive up next to me and Bob made a hand signal for me to follow them. I knew we were there when we stopped next to the sharpest jet airplane I had ever seen in my life. And to think, that this was his private plane. The engines were roaring, the stairs were down and the co-pilot was standing there waiting for Mr. DeNiro.

We got out and Todd opened the trunk to take Bob's luggage to the jet. Bob approached me, stopped a foot in front of me, and said, "Cos, I don't think anyone ever helped me like you did, and I can't thank you enough." Bob told me that there are people you observe all the time, but the ones you remember, you put in the back of your head and you don't forget them, ever! He gave me a "hug" and we said good-bye. As Robert DeNiro boarded that

Photo of Robert DeNiro in uniform. The insription says "Bill, Thanks
for everything, my friend. Take Care! Bob"

white twin engine jet, that morning it was like time was standing still, he turned in the doorway of the plane and waved to Todd and I.

I drove the fire car to the northeast corner of the airport and got out. Looking down the runway, I could see the jet roaring down the runway and, as it flew over me, I watched it jet into the early morning sun. I felt an emptiness that I had never felt before. Robert DeNiro was gone for now, but he would return in October to shoot the funeral procession.

October 5, 1990

Robin Chambers from New York called to tell me that Bob—or Mr. DeNiro—would be back in Chicago the night of October 6th. "Bob will call you when he arrives in Chicago," she said.

I received the call from Bob at about 9:00 P.M. We talked for about half an hour.

"How is the fire department and OFI?" he asked. "Have you had any big fires?"

I told him, "The only big fires we have had are the ones that Ron Howard is starting in this movie, *Backdraft*."

We both laughed at that one.

He said that we had to be at the movie set at 5:00 A.M., and that his trailer would be parked on Wabash, between Monroe and Adams. Also, that he was real tired and was looking to get some sleep. He thanked me again for being there for him, and I told him I would not miss it for anything!

Funeral Procession 0500 Hours
October 7, 1990

It was raining out and, for Ron Howard, it was the best thing

84

that could have happened.

I knocked on the trailer door and Ilona opened it. She was very happy to see me. We kissed each other like friends would. When I stepped into the trailer, Bob came over.

We looked at each other for a moment and then gave each other a big "hug" and pat on the back. I told him how much I missed working with him, that I'd had a trophy made for him with a fireman carrying a child down a ladder. It was bronze colored, on a wooden base, and the bronze plate on the front said,

Robert DeNiro
Actor/Investigator
Movie *Backdraft*
From your good friend "COS"

Bob said, "Thank you. This will be placed in my trophy case at the office."

As he was getting ready, as always, he asked me questions, this time about funerals. "Do you always wear the class "A" uniform?" he asked.

"Yes, with white shirts and white gloves."

Bob was admiring all the ribbons on my uniform, and Ilona said, "These are like yours."

Bob responded, "But Cos won his by saving people from fires." He then asked me how many people I had saved.

"Personally, I can say I saved fourteen people."

A knock came on the door and someone said, "Ten minutes, Mr. DeNiro."

I was close to the door and said, "OK."

Bob had to wear an arm sling because he had been injured saving Billy and Swayzak's (J. T. Walsh) lives when he was blown out of the building.

He asked me, "Do you know how this works?" We adjusted the sling, so it looked OK, but Ilona made sure by checking the photos.

As we got out of the trailer, there were a lot of people on the sidewalk. It was raining and Todd had the white caddie right there next to the trailer. Bob said to me, "You ride with me and stay by me all day."

I climbed into the back seat next to Bob, and Ilona was in the front seat.

As the car drove up Michigan Avenue, Bob could not believe how many firemen showed up in uniform and in the rain. We stopped at Washington Street, which was where Ron Howard was. Bob talked to Ron for a minute and then we rode up to the Wrigley Building.

Bob said, "Cos, you lead and I will be right behind you, so we stay in step."

The procession stepped off and we marched in the rain, from the Wrigley Building north of the Chicago River, to Jackson Boulevard which is about ten city blocks. The procession marched down Michigan Avenue four times. After the third time, we turned around at Adams Street and a little boy about ten years old with a broken arm came up to the car. I got out to see what he wanted and he asked if Mr. DeNiro would sign the cast on his arm. I asked Bob, and he opened the door and asked the little boy, with concern and tender-hearted compassion, how he had broken his arm. Then he signed the cast.

When the day was done, there was a party at the Green Door Bar for all the firemen. They were going to raffle off the 1990 Chrysler that had been used in the movie.

It was about 4:00 P.M. and still raining. Bob asked me if I was going to the party at the Green Door.

I said no, that I had to go to a fund raiser for Cook County Sheriff Michael Sheahan, who was a very good friend from when we were kids.

Back in the trailer, we had a drink or two and Bob said that he might want to go to the fund raiser.

I said, "Sure," that I would take him and bring him back.

He said to call him later at the Ritz. Ilona gave me the number and my call sheet for the next day and we left together.

I called him about 6:00 P.M. He said he was tired and that we had an early call the next day at the cemetery.

Graceland Cemetery –
Clark & Irving Park Road
October 8, 0500 Hours

I was told at the gate that Mr. DeNiro's trailer was east of the scene, about in the center of the cemetery.

Bob was already there when I arrived at the trailer and his son, Raphael, was also there. Bob said that they would leave right from the cemetery to the airport, when they were done shooting.

We had coffee and talked about the cemetery, that so many famous people were buried there. The tombstones were 25 feet high all around the pond where the trailer was parked. The scene was of two coffins lying side by side, each draped with the Chicago flag and with the fire helmets placed on the top. There was a honor guard of over one hundred firemen. The rain was still falling, but not hard and it took time to assemble all the firemen.

Then they called for Mr. DeNiro. We put our overcoats on and walked over to the set. On the way over, Bob was asking me about the code of signals and 3-3-5, which he was to bang out on the large bell.

I explained that it meant that a company was back in quarters, but that I had never heard it at a funeral before.

Bob took his place next to the bell, but I stayed down on the

The Red and Black sedan that Robert DeNiro and the author
used in the movie and the filtration plant.

road out of the way of the camera because the technical advisor
is not supposed to be in the movie.

All of a sudden, Bob called me and I just looked at him as he
walked down the embankment and said, "I want you to stand by
me up here."

So I started up the embankment, and as I did, the crew and
firemen started to cheer. It was a good feeling.

We were talking and laughing, when Ron walked over and
said, "This is a funeral. No laughing." But he was also laughing,
as he walked down to the road and........"ACTION!"

We did the scene about 10 times, and after lunch we did the
honor guard salute about 10 times in the rain. It was cold. Each
time we did the scene we lost a lot of firemen. They just were too
cold and wet.

Bob asked me to escort him to the airport again. He said,
"Ilona is having some boxes of my wardrobe from the movie
brought here."

I told Bob I no longer had the movie sedan. "I have my own
van here and can take whatever you have to the airport."

He looked at me and said, "Cos, you're the best!"

Bob invited Billy Baldwin and Ron Howard over for a good-bye drink. Ilona, as always, set up, and the five of us toasted Bob, Ron and the movie *Backdraft*.

One of the most amazing things about Robert DeNiro was illustrated while we were all standing inside his trailer talking and laughing rather loud. Bob heard his son Raphael ask a question while all of this was going on, and he answered him. The most amazing part was that none of us had heard him ask the question. To appreciate this, you would have to have been there! He was always attentive to his son, the entire time; it was great!

We loaded all of the boxes into the back of my van. Bob had a good friend that would be flying back to New York with him, and he asked me if there was enough room in my van.

I said, "Sure."

Bob's friend asked him, "Is this guy a good driver?"

He said, "Cos is the best driver. Don't worry about him. We went to many fires together, throughout Chicago, with the lights and siren."

Ilona asked me what way we would be taking because she was in my van, but wanted to tell Todd, who was driving Bob in the white caddie, to follow.

It was raining and cold, and we were all tired. We took Lake Shore Drive to the Stevenson Expressway.

We reached Midway Airport about 5:00 P.M., and entered in off of Central Avenue through the security gate, and then proceeded to that sharp looking white jet. It was still raining, as it had been for two days.

Then the ground crew came out to unload the van and the caddie. I got out to open the rear door of my van and a man held an umbrella over me. I looked over to see Bob being hustled onto the jet. My heart missed a beat I think. No good-bye. When I closed the doors on the van, the man who was holding the umbrella over me said, "Come on, Mr. DeNiro wants you to board the jet."

I said, "I am not going."

He said, "Mr. DeNiro just wants to say a personal good-bye."

Bob was standing in the doorway of the jet, yelling to me, "Come on, Cos," through the pouring rain.

I walked over and up a small stairway, into Bob's jet.

He grabbed me and said, "Come in and sit down. We have been grounded because of the rain." A flight attendant gave me a towel to dry my face and Bob said, "Get Cos a beer."

We laughed and I said, "Don't close that door!"

When Bob escorted me through this beautiful jet, I saw that the seats, about twenty of them, were of a brown leather and very comfortable. Bob called, "Hey, Cos, do you want some egg rolls? I will send out?"

How had all of this happened?

We sat around and told stories about the fires we had been at for about 45 minutes.

The pilot said, "We have a clearance to take off now."

I stood up.

Ilona was first to hug me and kiss me and said, "Thank you so much, Billy, for all you did. We will miss you. Please come to see us. Good-bye!"

Raphael came forward to shake my hand and we said good-bye.

Bob DeNiro was between me and the door and he said, "Cos, we're not going to let you go. You are going with us." He sounded like he meant it but we laughed, hugged for a long time and then we said good-bye!

I went to the end of the runway again and watched as the jet taxied down the runway, and a moment later they went screaming over my head.

May God Speed!